Pono

Pono:
A Hawaiian-Style Approach to Balance and Well-Being

Kaʻala Souza

Pono: A Hawaiian-Style Approach to Balance and Well-Being

Hi-Mountain Publishing

Copyright © 2012 Ka'ala Souza

Cover Photo Illustration courtesy of Charlie Osborn / www.hiartgallery.com © 2012 Charlie Osborn. Mahalo, Charlie!

Much appreciation to Gail Honda of Global Optima, Inc. for her invaluable work editing this book. All mistakes are mine and snuck in *after* her final edit.

Bible verses taken from the KING JAMES VERSION and the THE HOLY BIBLE, NEW INTERNATIONAL VERSION®, NIV® Copyright © 1973, 1978, 1984, 2011 by Biblica, Inc.™ Used by permission. All rights reserved worldwide.

All rights reserved. No part of this publication may be reproduced, stored in a retrieval system, or transmitted, in any form or in any means – by electronic, mechanical, photocopying, recording or otherwise – without prior written permission. But that's easy to obtain so no worries. Aloha!

Printed in the United States of America.

Ka'ala Souza
Visit my website at www.kaala.com

ISBN: 0985704608
ISBN-13: 978-0-9857046-0-5

To Leesa, my wife, for always believing.

CONTENTS

Introduction 1

Part I: Seeing 7

    Nothing New Here 14

    Hula Dancers, Maitais and Values 15

    This Place and This Time 18

    The Coconut Tree 19

    These Three Things 20

PART II: Place 25

  The Gift of Place 27

  A Sense of Place is 29

    No Place To Run, No Place to Hide 31

    Belonging 33

  Way-Finding Your Place 35

    I Failed Math But Read This Anyway 37

    Meaningful People 38

    Meaningful Places 38

    Heart and Head Analysis 39

    Hoʻomau—To Perpetuate 40

    The Oasis of Place 42

PART III: Purpose 45

Moving to Focus 47

Did He Just Call Me a Jackass?? 49

Bruce Lee's One-Inch Power Punch 51

A Sense of Purpose is 53

#1: Passion 55

The Intersection of Gladness and Hunger 57

#2: Kākou-Focused 58

Purposeful Discovery 61

You'll See it When You Know it 62

Death As a Guest Lecturer 64

Who are You and What are You Doing Here? 68

The Pono Q&As 69

Follow Your Passions, Find Your Purpose 69

Joy Unlimited 72

PART IV: Power 77

Hurricanes And Flat Surf 79

A Sense of Power Is 81

Happy Happens 87

Happy Test 88

What Happy is NOT 89

C'mon get happy!! 91

Six Getting Happy Principles 92

Happy is a Skill 95

Some Specific Don'ts 103

Pono Strong 109

Kalalau: Crawl In, Swim Out? 110

Re-CREATE-ion 113

Zombie Preppers 117

Pono as Rx'd 123

Physical Strength: If You Can Run, You Won't Have to Hide 123

Mental Strength: More of Less 128

Relational Strength: Be a Groomer Not a Fighter 132

Spiritual Strength: Sandwiches and Skinny Jeans 137

Overcoming the DO-DOs 143

You Must Be the Goose 147

PART V: Being 151

Are We Pono? 153

Bottles and Shovels 157

I have come that they may have life,
and that they may have it more abundantly.
—John 10:10

INTRODUCTION

Aia no ka pane i loko iho no.
The answer lies deep within us.

Don't these cryptic quotes drive you nuts? The answer to what? *What's* inside of me, answering *what* deep question?!?

The question this Hawaiian proverb answers is you.

Well, that clears it up. Not.

Really.

You are the question and the answer deeply affects your life. Who are you? Where do you come from? What does your future hold? The good news is that the answer to the question of "you" is already there. The bad news is that it's buried deep. Who you are is definitely not laying on the surface or hanging low on the tree.

Your ability to find the answer, to get deep, determines your destiny—and ultimately, the quality of the rest of your life.

Speaking of quality of life, what is it that you want?

Think about it. In this one life we have, what do you want? Security? Money? Health? Love? Nice house/car/boat and/or other "stuff"? What's on your list? What you want may be a key to understanding who you are. Or, to put it a little differently: you are what you want.

I believe the seeds of identity were planted in us from the beginning and one of our major jobs in life is nurturing and bringing these seeds to fruition.

If we are unable to do this, our future, in every sense, is limited and marked by suffering.

Our relationships, well-being, friends and families suffer.

Our careers, jobs and ability to produce wealth suffer.

Even our health suffers.

All this because we can't find the answer—even though it's within us; all this because of our inability to get deep enough.

Wow. Can you find a gloomier introduction?

But of course there's hope, right? A plan to save us all? A pill that will open the doors to a paradise found?

Sort of.

One author says that "You have to 'Be' before you can 'Do' and 'Do' before you can 'Have.'" This 'be-ing' requires mental and emotional labor—basically, work. So far, there's no pill out there that we can swallow, sit back and have our 'be-ing' happen; we have to work at the be-ing so we can get to the have-ing.

There is a step before the "Be" mentioned above and it's "See." You have to see before you can be. You must be able to identify certain key elements in your future and your past, to see them, before you be and do and have.

It doesn't come from focusing on our careers, making money or even our families. Those things are by-products of being. The health and wealth that accrue (or doesn't) come as a result of a proper (or improper) perspective.

There is a right order, a right way and a right approach to this, to find this and to see this.

This way is called *pono* and it helps us to see rightly and it makes all the difference.

***Pono* is...**
Pono is right and, like many other Hawaiian words, it's deep, multi-faceted and means lots of different things to lots of different people. The word is simple enough to explain to a child yet still so complex that you can spend a lifetime searching for understanding and barely scratch the surface.

Pono is apparent and unmistakable yet difficult to define. It's one of those things that you just know it when you see it, or maybe more instructively, when you feel it. Defining *pono* is like trying to explain the sweet spot in tennis or golf to someone. Words just don't seem sufficient to the task. When you hit it your whole body knows it. *Pono* just feels—right.

Pono is something you do, it's something you are and it's something you live.

The dictionary definition includes concepts of goodness, rightness and moral correctness. *Pono* is righteousness, what is proper. It's also a sense of completeness, of things that are in their proper place, of balance and alignment, of doing the right thing, choosing the proper way.

When you're living *pono* all the elements that make up your life — your family, job, health, relationships—are in the right place. There is powerful alignment in what you believe, say and do.

Pono is the life, that wonderful life, you were meant to live.

What a Wonderful (Blind) World

As I listen to Louis Armstrong sing of his wonderful world (or more recently, Israel Kamakawiwoʻole's version with solo ukulele) I can see the colors, the trees, the roses, the skies of blue and it's beautiful. The song gives us a picture, a vision, of what is, or maybe even, what is not quite yet.

To have vision is to have a picture of the future, to see what is yet to be and what the possibilities may be. The bible says that "without vision people perish" and the presence of it may be one of the single most powerful determining factors of a successful life.

Helen Keller, herself blind, said that the most pathetic person in the world, the one to be pitied the most, is "someone who has sight, but no vision."

This book is about seeing, truly seeing, your life. And once you're able to see, it's about helping balance and align your life to bring your vision of the future to reality.

For many of us balance is the frantically sought after Holy Grail. Juggling work, children, spouses, friends, exercise, getting dinner ready and the kids to their class, paying the bills and everything else that we have to do every minute on the minute consumes our every moment.

The lack of balance is no joke. Check out the statistics on families and divorces, look at the waistlines and bank accounts of the people around you. Look in the mirror.

Everywhere we turn we see people settling for less and thinking that's the best it gets. We are desperate—desperate for something that we have a difficult time even describing. We know in our gut that life isn't just the quantity and it isn't just the quality. Can't it be both? Is it even possible?

Looking for solutions in books, pills, and esoteric gurus leads us to trying out the newest this or more of that. We start with the best intentions of prioritizing and balancing only to watch the promises we made to ourselves slowly disappear under oceans of wasted time and effort. Frankly, this book is no different than any other. There are no lifeboats here, no easy rescues. We are all in the deep end and we all have to learn to swim.

The sad thing is that many of us don't even recognize that we are drowning, we're going down.

It was Thoreau who said "The mass of men lead lives of quiet desperation," and we are those quietly desperate, submerging without a cry, without a splash, without a struggle, without a sigh.

This is still a beautiful, wonderful world but maybe we're too blind to see it. *Pono* is the key to help us unlock and open the eyes of our heart.

The answer for your well-being is, and always will be, a *pono* you.

KAʻALA SOUZA

PART I: *SEEING*

"Where there is no vision the people perish."
—Proverbs 29:18

"The question is not what you look at,
but what you see."
–Henry D. Thoreau

He 'ike 'ana ia i ka pono.
It is a recognizing of the right thing.
One has seen the right thing to do
and has done it.
—Mary Kawena Pukui

KAʻALA SOUZA

1
EYES WIDE OPEN

I had never performed CPR on a person before that day. Yeah, I had gone through the training and certifications but never had I been face to face (literally) with a situation requiring me to use it.

Before I tell you about this let me tell you first that I am that guy. You know the one. That person who had some terminal illness, near-death experience and/or other life-changing encounter that changed his life and now he feels this big need to try and help other people. We've all heard of these kind of stories, right?

I didn't want to be that guy—who would?? But the experience(s) fundamentally changed my fundamentals and now I am almost compelled to do what I do.

Back to the story...

At the time of this CPR experience I was working as a marketing researcher in Honolulu after resigning my position as a full-time associate pastor. I had been in the ministry for over ten years and wasn't thinking of stopping anytime soon. It wasn't a planned resignation; in fact, it wasn't even a pleasant one. I was disillusioned and the church I worked for was frustrated. Things had come to a head and I'd quit in anger and disappointment, shocked that what I had thought was a lifelong mission was at an end.

This resignation left me struggling to deal with an abrupt change of calling, meaning and purpose in my life. As a pastor I was clear on my role in the world. I existed to serve and to help. In my new job as market researcher I gathered data and ran program evaluations. Hmm…My life had become detached from something I thought solid. I was drifting, searching, looking for something to hook up and anchor to.

Our family decided to take a vacation on the island of Hawai'i, the Big Island. On our camping trip we visited an incredibly beautiful, very remote beach at the end of Pololū Valley that required a thirty minute hike down a mountain trail to reach the start of the beach.

On the way down I kept repeating an 'oli, a Hawaiian chant that had repeated a request for wisdom and knowledge. Over and over I chanted this, not seriously as a request, but more like a way to pass the time. Be careful what you ask for!

We had only been at the bottom of the trail for a few minutes when our attention was drawn to a guy running up the beach towards us, waving, shouting, and pointing out towards the waves. In Hawai'i, that's *always* a bad body language combination.

As we hurried to meet him, he told us that someone had been swept out by the rip current and needed help immediately.

My brother-in-law Tom and I rushed down the beach to where a couple of teenagers and a woman with a small baby were gathered. It was a visiting family on the last day of their vacation and the person out there was the kids' father and the woman's husband. Terrified, they were watching three people who had gone out to try to rescue him struggle to make their way back to shore, caught in the same powerful current that had swept the man out to sea.

In between crashing waves, I caught one brief glimpse of the guy a half-mile off shore.

We looked around the beach for something to use as a flotation device. The waves were big that day, hence the strong rip current, and no one wanted to go out in that torrent without some kind of flotation device or support and risk getting caught in it ourselves.

We found nothing—not even a discarded air mattress or surfboard.

I started walking out into the ocean with Tom. As soon as we reached knee-deep water I knew we were in trouble, too. The current and conditions looked bad from the beach but were even worse once in the water. Tom looked at me and said that he would go back on the beach and guide me.

I started out, half-wading, half-swimming as the water grew deeper, looking back at the beach for directions. It wasn't hard getting out, in fact it was way too easy since the current was moving in that direction. I knew that coming back in, against that current, was going to be the problem.

Just as I reached the inside of the breakers, I came upon the body of the man, floating facedown in the water. The waves had pushed his limp body closer to shore. Turning him over, I immediately kicked for the beach, trying to use the waves that were pushing in to help against the current pushing out.

When I finally made it to shore, before I could even get out of the water, my wife and Tom waded in and began to do rescue breathing. I prayed and helped pull the guy up on the sand while Tom, an Army medic, and my wife, a critical care nurse, alternated the compressions and breathing.

I did CPR for the first time that day, and the only time since, as we took turns praying, breathing, and compressing. All the while the man's two teenaged sons circled around us crying with his wife standing at his feet, holding their baby girl, begging us not to stop.

The man's eyes were wide open the entire time. Occasionally, ocean water and pizza from his lunch would dribble out the side of his mouth but we never got a pulse.

We worked on him for about forty-five minutes until an emergency services helicopter arrived and took him to the hospital.

It was a silent and anxious hike back up the hill with the family. Our exhausted, post-adrenalin-filled bodies felt ready to drop. At the top my wife and I drove with the family in their rental car to the hospital where we sat and waited for the doctor's report. I declined their offer of a slice of pizza.

As we waited we talked. Turns out that this was the final day of their vacation and they wanted to take one last tour, one last drive around the island. The couple had renewed their marriage vows earlier that morning and were hoping for some nice beach pictures to finish out their trip.

Twenty minutes after we arrived the doctor came out and announced that the man didn't make it. It was devastating. I remember the wife immediately screaming and one of the boys throwing a chair against the wall, the baby crying and a room full of despair. I didn't know what to do and just sat there, numb.

The doctor told them that he could contact a chaplain if they desired, which they did.

And here my life changed, or rather, the understanding of my life changed.

My wife raised her hand, called out and said that there was no need for that because her husband was a pastor and he could help.

I looked at her shocked and dumbfounded—I was a marketing researcher, I told her, and definitely not a pastor. I quit and wasn't doing that kind of stuff anymore. I kind of bumped her and tried to pull her hand down. She looked at me, just stared at me, and said, "I don't care what you think you are or what you think you've become, but inside, in that real part of you, you're a pastor, you help people and this is what you do."

"But what am I supposed to say," I asked?

"You're the pastor; you'll figure it out," was all she said.

Thanks.

I raised my hand, nodded, and said, "Yeah, I can help," and walked into the emergency room with the family. I actually don't remember much of what happened. I know I ended up not saying much at all, just hugging and crying and praying and crying with them. Lots of tears, lots of tears.

Hours later we drove back to our campsite and debriefed with the rest of our family who had been waiting anxiously for news. We sat around the campfire and told the story over and over, trying to cope and deal with what happened that day. To say it was traumatic would be an understatement. When I went to sleep that night I could still see the man's eyes looking blankly up at us as we were on the beach. In fact, I can still see his face right now as I write this.

Weeks later, months later in fact, I came to recognize that no matter what my job happened to be at the time, my calling was to help and serve people by sharing whatever strengths or gifts I had been given.

It took happenings of this magnitude to see, then once I saw, to know. I don't believe one needs to go through situations like this before seeing and knowing are possible and I hope you never to have to. This book is written with more questions than answers hoping to give you more opportunity to examine life and arrive at your own conclusions.

Nothing New Here
Before we get much further in this book let me be upfront with you: there's nothing new here. No unusual or innovative insights. No fresh-off-the-shelf guru help offered. I haven't been sitting on a mountaintop meditating and coming up with new ideas.

What I'm writing about are old things. They've been passed on to me from my family, my friends, my teachers and mentors, who in their turn, received it from others. It's been handed down through proverbs, sayings, and stories —old proverbs, sayings and stories.

There's nothing new here but there is something solid.

It's this heaviness of that which comes with time, the weight of this past-ness, that provides security in a very insecure world, stability in shaky times.

There's something found in the yesterdays that seems lost in today's cult of newness.

"You've gotta see this best new movie of the season!"

"There's a new book out from (insert author's name)."

"Have you heard that new song?"

"That's so old. Why don't you get a new one?"

"Here's a new _____ for you. Guaranteed to get you to lose weight, get rich, AND find the person of your dreams —before lunch!"

"Want to know how to find yourself? Here's a new ___ to help you!"

With this mindset, new always equates to better.

I've never been OK with this "out with the old, in with the new" mentality. I'm not against new things at all and I'm not a luddite. What I am about is balance and fullness and that doesn't necessarily come with newness.

I'm about life that's lived completely, fully, abundantly. If there's something out there, new or old, that can help me make this happen, that's what I want. My goal is to share perspectives that I believe can help you find and live this balance and fullness.

Hula Dancers, Maitais and Values

Many of these perspectives come from the culture and place that I'm from. Here in the Hawaiian islands, the most remote island group in the world, we, by necessity, do things differently. This obviously affects our thinking and approach to life, in what I think, is a very positive and powerful way.

A nationwide Gallup survey in 2011 ranked Hawai'i residents first in terms of well-being and happiness for the third year in a row.

An article referencing the report flippantly asked if warm weather and beautiful beaches were the key to happiness. I'm not denying sun and ocean are awesome but I think it's more than that. The key is found more in the values and attitudes than the sand and surf.

Many people look at Hawai'i as a vacation paradise filled with hula dancers, grass shacks and endless supplies of tropical drinks, served to you by ukulele playing natives. Once past the glitzy tourist traps the heart of our islands beats a little differently.

As the proverbial "melting pot of the Pacific" we are a hodgepodge of East and West, a collection of multicultural values and beliefs that have blended together to produce something wonderfully rich, vibrant and tangibly alive. These values, whether we're conscious of them or not, affect our attitudes which in turn affect our actions and behaviors. Recognizing and cultivating the key foundational values can make the difference between a fulfilling life or an empty life.

When I talk about balance and well-being there are several Hawaiian values that lend themselves to a Western mind. *Aloha*, *lōkahi* and *pono* all provide rich meaning and depth to the concept of ordering and arranging our existence. Generally, you can come up with a denotative, or dictionary meaning of the words, but to truly understand them you must try to live them.

Our sense of well-being is directly related to the interplay of these values in our lives.

Aloha

Aloha is almost synonymous with Hawai'i, the "Aloha State." When you ask what it means you get a lot of different answers—and to me, all correct in their context. Hello, goodbye, greetings, love, compassion, mercy, kindness and giving. I've even had people tell me that it means to eat together (no doubt a lot of aloha is shared around the table!).

Aloha means different things to people because most experienced it before they defined it. We associate the word with feelings and actions and you can always tell when someone has it—or they don't.

Lōkahi

In *lōkahi* we have an understanding of oneness, of unity and togetherness. E-kahi in Hawaiian is the numeral one. To lō-kahi or lo'o-kahi is to cause to become one. This is a powerful concept of interdependence and teamwork. I need you and you need me. We are incomplete without each other and are all essential parts of the ecosystem of our lives. When I'm living in harmony with everything around me I'm living *lōkahi*.

While both *aloha* and *lōkahi* do speak to balance and abundance in our lives our focus is *pono*.

Pono

Ua mau ke ea o ka 'āina i ka pono.
The life of the land is perpetuated in righteousness.

This is the Hawaiian state motto. We can understand this not only as an island state but also as individuals. Our life will have life, will be a full life, as it continues, as it's perpetuated in *pono*.

When King Kamehameha III spoke this in 1843 in a time of political crisis it became the motto of the Hawaiian kingdom. His hope was that his people, so closely linked to the land, to the *'āina*, would continue to grow and develop in a period of disruptive and tumultuous change.

I can imagine the King, looking out over the islands, recognizing the impact increased contact with the West would bring, knowing that the tangible changes occurring in the land must have corresponding cultural support to protect the values that protect the lives. He may have been pondering the question, the same question we are asking, of how to keep our life abundant and meaningful in the face of scarcity and ambiguity.

When I think of land that's alive I think of growth, vitality, energy and abundance. A land alive is a land complete and whole, and it shows in both tangible and intangible ways. We can feel the life on levels we can't always understand or quantify.

At the other end of the continuum, on the dead end, we find the opposite. Here the land is cold, it's retreating, it's empty, sterile and dull. There's a sense of incompleteness, of something missing, that just brushes up against our psyche and creates a chill in our souls. We can feel this as well and it doesn't feel good.

The life in the land, the "ea," only continues when it continues to move in a right way, in *pono*. It can only be perpetuated in righteousness, in correctness. To maintain and even grow, the land and its people must remain firmly aligned in *pono*.

Our life is meant to be lived the same way, with everything in the right place. Think of it as

Ua mau ke ea YOUR LIFE i ka PONO.
Your life is perpetuated in righteousness.

This Place and This Time

A while back I was speaking on finding your future at a church retreat for people in college and those just getting started in their careers. I don't recall what I spoke on (yikes—it was a really long time ago) but I do remember one young guy coming up to me after my presentation and telling me something that absolutely floored me.

He had just graduated from college and was about to start his teaching career. Excited and passionate about the future he told me something I've never forgotten.

He said, "Right now, in this place, in this time, I'm right where God wants me to be and doing what I'm supposed to be doing."

Wow.

In one profound statement he told me where he was at, what he was doing and where he was going. I was (almost) speechless. It was striking for me because I couldn't make as bold a statement at the time and I was the speaker at the conference.

We spoke for a little bit more before I mumbled something like "Hey, that's great. Uh, good luck," and casually (but quickly) moved off.

What a concept!

To be able to say that this place where I'm at right now is exactly where I need to be and this thing that I'm doing is what I'm supposed to be doing is incredibly powerful. This is *pono*. When you can make this type of statement, and live in it, you are experiencing what living *pono* is, being in balance with the important things in your life.

The Coconut Tree

At the sadly opposite end of this spectrum was Kawika. Kawika was a teen-ager, maybe a sophomore or junior in high school when I first met him. We got together after he had some run-ins with the police and his Auntie had run out of options (and patience!) and asked if I could counsel him.

We met at his home and it wasn't easy. Those intro-type moments where he knows that I know and I know that he knows make for awkward times. As we spoke I tried probing for some sense of where he was coming from, what motivated him, what he was about. We talked about his family, talked about his friends. I asked him about his hobbies and he muttered back "stuff." I asked how school was and he just grunted.

Finally, as he got past some of the initial edginess we started talking about the future and what he was expecting and anticipating. He perked up when I asked him what he enjoyed doing and said that being with his friends, cruising, and drinking beer at the park, under the coconut tree—just, you know, "hanging out"—got him stoked.

This was, at the time, the most important thing he could think of, his most important place to be. Collectively, the full extent of his life's vision, didn't extend too much past the shadow of this one coconut tree.

His Auntie called a month or so after Kawika and I met and said he had been picked up by the police and put into the youth correctional facility. We visited him there and continued to talk. When I asked him what he wanted to do when he got out, still trying to figure out what he thought of his future, he said he most wanted to see his friends and hang out in their spot under the tree.

That was the last time I saw him. His Auntie called me a few weeks after this, checking to see if I had heard from him. Turns out he had escaped, ran off and the police were looking for him.

I found out later that they caught him, close by his home. Guess where? Yep, with his friends, cruising, drinking beer, under that coconut tree.

The shadow line of that tree was the full extent of Kawika's vision.

Something was missing there, some ingredient that wasn't added, some part not installed in his system. His was a life not drawing from an awareness of where he came from or where he would go; there was no future for him. The vision he had for his life was, to say nicely, limited. It is probably more accurate to say stunted and myopic. His vision, or maybe his lack of vision represented by that tree, was his cage.

If we're being honest, many of us miss these things as well. We have our own safe, confining coconut trees. I have seen it in and all around me in the stressed out, unhappy, overworked, unmotivated, out-of-shape, no future, no hope, no vision people everywhere.

These Three Things

If I had a chance today there are three essential elements I would work to get Kawika to see, three things that I would make sure he got before I would leave him. Three things that could help him move out from the shadow of that tree and into a more fulfilling life.

First, I would want him to know where he came from to give him a foundation to move from. Then I would want him to know where he was going to give him a direction to move toward. Lastly, I would want him to know how to find the motivation and the strength to keep moving until he got there.

These three things I call a

> *Sense of Place*
>
> *Sense of Purpose*
>
> *Sense of Power*

Each is captured more in essence and feel than data or tests and all three are essential for fullness in our lives. If we have Place without Purpose we are left holding on to an empty bag full of what was. Purpose without Place gives us a driven, consumed and overly high view of self. Finally, Place and Purpose without Power fades and leaves unrealized potential in its wake. *Pono* happens when all three are present and balanced in our lives.

So, how do we find and implement the three and live life *pono*? Let's begin, of course, at the beginning by looking back and identifying the place we come from. The next section will define and help you examine your *Sense of Place*.

HIGHLIGHTS

Life is more than just surviving and barely making it! Our quality of life is determined largely by the depth of our soul and character.

To go deeper we must "be" before we "do" or "have" and this requires work.

Vision is about the possibilities in your life. Without vision people perish.

Pono is the life you were meant to live. *Pono* is both the ends and the means for achieving balance in life.

Your life will have life and continue, be perpetuated, in that life, only inasmuch as you are able to maintain balance.

To be balanced, to be complete, is to have a *Sense of Place*, a *Sense of Purpose* and a *Sense of Power*.

QUESTIONS

1. On a scale of 1-10, how balanced is your life?

2. Does your life more closely resemble a living, vibrant, growing 'āina or a cold, dull, sterile piece of property?

3. Where does your life stand when held up to the definition of *pono* as rightness, goodness, and moral correctness?

4. Are you able to say that the place you're at right now is the place you're supposed to be? Why or why not?

5. The coconut tree was both a physical and metaphorical symbol of limitations for Kawika. What is the metaphor for you? What keeps you from reaching further and dreaming bigger?

KAʻALA SOUZA

PART II: *PLACE*

"When you know who you are,
you know what to do."
–George Emery

To become different from what we are,
we must have some awareness
of what we are.
—Eric Hoffer

KAʻALA SOUZA

2
THE GIFT OF PLACE

"Tell everybody who your grandpa is."—Francis Meyer

I was the presiding minister at funeral of my grandfather, Francis Hyde Kalanihonohoumakou Meyer—definitely one of the hardest ceremonies I've done. The service was a strain emotionally, physically, spiritually. I never realized how difficult it was to speak coherently through sobs and tears. I also didn't realize, until that day, what my grandfather meant when he told me to "tell everybody" about him.

I grew up with my grandparents—they raised me and loved the heck out of me. My grandfather taught me how to swim and how to surf, drove me to the beach and to the ballpark, and spent countless hours encouraging and teaching me. He taught me how to drive. (My wife even says to this day that I drive like a grandpa.) He was, and always will be, the single most influential person in my youth. I guess he was technically my grandfather but in every other way he was my father.

I met my actual, biological father when I was about 30 years old. I arrived at the restaurant early, watching people come in, wondering if I would even recognize the man who was my father. Men would come in the door and I would search their faces for some clue, some indication, some connection.

When he arrived we sat, made small talk for a bit, and tried to get over the obvious awkwardness. One of the first things I told him was that, growing up, I never lacked for a father figure. I remember being fiercely protective of the role my grandfather played in my life. I also remember telling him that part of what I did lack, though, was a connection to his part of the family. It was something that I sensed as missing in my life.

I knew no one and nothing from my father's side. No cousins, no grandparents, no friends, no history, nothing. People would ask, "Hey, you related to this Souza or that Souza?" and almost before they finished the sentence I would interject and tell them they probably knew more Souzas than I did. Part of what made me Me wasn't there.

I never missed having my father in my life because my grandfather fulfilled that role in its entirety. I did miss, however, having a connection to that part of who I am, the history, the people and the places.

I've never been one of those who empathized with those television shows or books where a long-lost birth parent is sought after and found; they never appealed to me. My connection and place in this world, however, has always intrigued me. Where I belong and who I belonged with were questions I needed answers for.

It finally hit home, in a funeral hall full of his closest family and friends, that my grandfather had already given me a large part of the answer and wanted to give me more. What he wanted me to have was a connection, a direct line to him and from him. He wanted me to have a link, through his life, to the people and events of his life. He wanted to give me a sense of who I was and where I came from. He wanted me to have the gift of place.

3
A SENSE OF PLACE IS...

A *Sense of Place* is a sense of certainty. It is that identity that provides security and that security that provides identity. It's the roots. It's depth. It's that part way down inside that is connected to that which is outside. It's the foundation to build life upon.

When you have a *Sense of Place* there is a firmness to your soul, your past is steady and solid no matter how shifty the sands of your future. When there is no *Sense of Place* your soul's ability to stabilize is weakened and it wanders, lost and purposeless. There's no core strength without this base.

I believe that this foundation was missing in Kawika and his is a familiar story. Fatherless and motherless he became placeless. Or rather, he sought to "re-place," to fill what was missing through other people, situations and activities that offered him a sort of security and identity.

The friends he hung out with were other kids, many of whom were probably from single-parent homes as well, who were also missing this depth in their person. Together they did the best they could to piece together their collective remnants and create a place to belong. But it only extended so far from them and through them. Their efforts were limited because the source of this *re-placement* place was themselves.

When we are our own sun and moon and stars the universe is a very small, very shaky place. If our place is the shadow of a coconut tree we fear stepping out into the unknown. We are afraid to take chances and risks, to probe life's possibilities, because we lack the lifeline of place.

Our *Sense of Place* is the

...**awareness** of our role in the grand scheme of things.

...**acceptance** of our responsibilities in this life.

... **acknowledgement** of the relationships that have created us, that have made us, that are a part of us.

A *Sense of Place* that comes from self is too small to stabilize our lives. If you've ever tried balancing on a too-narrow surfboard in large surf you'll know what I mean. If not, imagine trying to walk across a balance beam while a group of people throw water balloons at you. It's much easier to balance on a surfboard (and a beam) when the base is wider, and in the case of our lives, deeper.

You can see it in our society's insecurities and uncertainties. The most insecure people, communities, and even countries are the ones without the strong base found in a *Sense of Place*.

Think about it. Do you remember that blustering bully that teased you back in elementary school? The one that never missed an opportunity to put you down or intimidate you? Looking back do you really think he was a secure person?

Or maybe you were that person. Did you behave from a position of strength or fear?

I have a lot of friends who are martial artists and I've found that the best, most skilled (and deadly) ones are also the most secure and humble. They know what they can do and see no need to posture or prove it to anyone.

The wars and threats of wars between countries or people groups have at their root an absence of place marked by intense insecurity.

Our personal fears are evident at work and at home. The divorce rate in America, and even the status of marriage itself, exhibits our inability to create and maintain deep relationships with others—which makes sense given we don't have the depth in ourselves.

Our insecurities identify the absence of place.

We're afraid of the shadows that chase us, not realizing that those shadows of our past are a part of us and we need to reclaim them if we want to have a chance at peace, at being *pono* with our self.

We have to work to move off our baser instincts and onto the platform of place.

No Place To Run, No Place to Hide

High-school. First day. New school. Freshman. I remember that first day of school, the anxiety, the questions, heck, the fear.

I was a newly made teenager and heading off to my first day of big-kid school. I made it through the first couple of periods OK; the first day's requirements weren't much more than listening to the teacher and saying "Here."

It was while heading off to lunch that it hit me: Where was I going to sit?!? I knew no one, no one knew me. I wasn't signed up for football or basketball (and wasn't planning to) nor was I a member of the math, chess or drama club. There was going to be NOWHERE to sit because I was nobody.

You ever have that kind of feeling? That square peg feeling? That, "One of these things does not belong here, one of these things is not quite the same" feeling?

I was sweating as I entered the cafeteria. By the time I had my tray of food I was about ready to drop it and run for home. Before me was a vast ocean of people who had no names and no reason to ask me mine. As I headed blindly, head down, into the crowd, walking I don't know where, hoping for an empty table, I heard a guy call out over the heavy drone of voices.

"You want to sit with us?"

Was he talking to me? I kept walking, but slowed down, hoping.

"Hey, you want to sit with us?" he repeated.

He was talking to me!

I mumbled something affirmative and sat down.

I ate—quickly and without hardly a word—said "Thanks," and left.

The next day at lunch I looked for the same group, found them, walked towards them still hoping, and upon seeing their positive recognition, sat down again. For the next two years I sat with people from this same group nearly every day. They became my friends and probably contributed more to my emerging adolescent identity than anyone or anything else at the time.

Without even knowing (who thinks like this in high school??) they gave me much more than a place to sit at lunch. To this day I thank them for a place to belong. *Mahalo*, Jay. I haven't forgotten.

Belonging

"It's important for us...when we honor our ancestors...it gives us a place, a place to belong."—Nainoa Thompson

A *Sense of Place* allows us to move forward confidently by providing an anchor point linking us to something larger than us. We aren't wandering aimlessly looking for a chair. Self-confidence and security are a by-product of a strong *Sense of Place*.

Too often, in our obsession with climbing up the vision and mission ladder for the future, we don't realize the need for a strong anchor at the base. A *Sense of Place*, though an abstract concept, acts as a solid concrete foundation for our lives. Because place connects us to where we come from and who we come from, we are kept from drifting aimlessly, pushed and pulled in whatever direction the wind blows and the currents flow.

Our place is unchanging and provides a center of reference much like the hub of a wheel. No matter how life twists and turns there's always a place for us to center on.

There's also a feeling of continuity that comes from place. Because there's no need to reinvent that wheel we can build upon what's come before.

In the pre-contact Hawaiian culture there was no written language but there were vast oral libraries passed down from generation to generation. All the sciences, all the histories—all transferred memory to memory, person to person. With each generation building upon the previous, the collective consciousness was codified, enlarged and strengthened.

When we recognize our history, good and bad, and stay tied to where we come from, we are strengthened in the same way.

KAʻALA SOUZA

4
WAY-FINDING YOUR PLACE

"I know my place but my place don't know me."
—Band of Skulls

Once we recognize the importance of and the need for our *Sense of Place* the question of how we find it surfaces. With something like this, that isn't tangible, we have a treasure that isn't findable. Really, there's probably no direct way to "find" it as much as there are ways to connect and intersect with it.

Years ago I was at a lecture that my wife's calabash uncle (close family friend) was giving on ancient Polynesian way-finding and navigation techniques. Fascinating stuff!

A Polynesian voyager could safely sail thousands of miles to a distant island and return to his homeland without the aid of modern navigational tools. Without what westerners would consider vital, necessary voyaging tools, Pacific Islanders were able to sail, navigate and populate the largest ocean in the world. This was deliberate and purposeful travel and not accidental, blown off course discovery.

Their strength was observation and discipline. Generations of watching and orienting to the signs around them in the sky, the ocean and the elements had created mental charts and maps of the Pacific. They had different techniques and methods for setting their course.

The early morning and evening, when the sun rose and set, were the most important times of the day for the navigator as they could know their relative direction according to the sun. At night, the memorized patterns of the stars provided locations and headings.

The movements and behaviors of birds, fish, and other ocean life were also indicators of location. Amazing! One of the things that my wife's uncle said that really stopped me, though, was that a navigator couldn't determine his present location by just looking up at the stars in the night sky. (Huh? I thought that's what it was all about?)

You can't know where you are now by looking at where you are now.

He went on to say that the navigator can only tell where they were on a particular night by comparing the stars currently overhead with their position on the previous night. Essentially, you had to remember where you'd been to know where you were. This floored me.

You can't know where you are now by looking at where you are now. It's true for Polynesian seafaring and absolutely relevant to our lives. This is profound.

Eventually, I recognized the importance of this for understanding who we are and where we're going as we navigate our own oceans of life. When we think of finding our *Sense of Place* it helps to look back, at the stars of last night and the nights previous, to remember how we became who we are.

I Failed Math But Read This Anyway

I'm no statistician so don't take me to your exam but I'm going to bring up the concept of trend-lines and linear regression analysis. When I say I'm not a mathematician I'm not joking or being modest and humble; my brain doesn't work like that. I can't explain how a trend-line analysis can do what it does; I just know it does.

I do it the non-old-fashioned way and put data points into columns and click the "trend-line analysis" button using my computer spreadsheet. The software then spits out a chart with my data points distributed vertically and horizontally with a "best-fit" line running through them. This is the trend-line. With this I can get a picture of where my data has been and, of more relevance to our discussion, where it's going.

Stay with me on this.

When the traditional Polynesian navigators compared their current night's star patterns with the previous they were, in effect, performing something like a linear regression to plot their trending direction. They could make course corrections or adjustments or stay their current course based on their position.

The reason I'm even bringing up something so far over my head is because it fits in this quest that we have to find where we come from to discover where we are going.

The challenge for us in connecting/intersecting with our *Sense of Place* is to find and input the data of people, places and events that have shaped us in the past to get a feel for where our future is heading. It's not fortune-telling, by any means. It is connecting the dots of our life and drawing a line to our future.

If we're on course, great. We stay on track, we hold to what we've been doing. If we find the trend pointing in a direction that is not where we want to go, we now have the information to make changes. Developing our *Sense of Place* first requires an awareness of it.

Meaningful People
Here's an activity for you to get started with your own life navigation. It's a chance to think, cogitate and meditate on the stars of your past.

Get a notepad or open up a word processor. At the top write: **People**.

Now, list two or three folks that have personally and directly contributed to who you are, how you think and how you act. Next to their names, describe some of the reasons why they made your list. What characteristics did they have that you admired? What did they do or say that stayed with you? How did they influence you?

That list was for people that you have interacted with directly. Now, make another of people you've read about, heard about or watched on screen that have had an impact on you as well. Answer the same questions for them.

The third, and final list for this section on finding place, deals with actual places and events in our lives.

Meaningful Places
For the Hawaiian people, there is *mana*, or spiritual power, in all things. Hawaiians have a concept, *wahi pana*, that describes a sacred or legendary place. This is a location where something momentous occurred or where there was much *mana*. We want to be able to identify those wahi pana in our own life.

At the top of a new page, write: **Places**.

When you think about places that are important to you what comes to mind? Are those places associated with important events or people? Remember those important events and remember where they happened.

List your places on the page.

Remember the pivotal places for you, the big events, the big happenings. Recall births, deaths, marriages, divorces, promotions, buyings, sellings, hirings, and firings. What places make you feel happy, sad, victorious or afraid?

Heart and Head Analysis
After reaching into our heart, let's analyze with our head. Do you see a trend developing? Are there characteristics that these people share that you think is important? Were all the people on your list positive influences? Or did some make the list by demonstrating how you would NOT want to live?

What about the places you listed? Out of all the possible locations and events these few made the list. Why? What stood out about them? What makes them important to you?

When we go back and reconnect in our heart and head with these people and places it opens us up to ourselves. This is good, no doubt but it may be emotionally difficult. We begin to stretch our souls a bit and, just like when I stretch to touch the ground, if I haven't practiced, it's tight and sometimes painful.

Don't push. Go slow. Ease into the stretch. No need to force it. It'll open on its own.

The benefits of a hamstring stretch and a place-identifying soul stretch are the same: increased flexibility and strength along with a fuller range of motion. A full range of motion physically describes what your body is fully capable of doing. When you get that same fullness in your soul you become complete, pulling the fragmented pieces of you together in deep, rich, wholeness. Strength is found in that wholeness.

I strongly recommend that you find someone to do this with and share these life-navigating discoveries and uncoveries. You don't have to analyze each other (in fact please don't!), just listen.

Now we can begin to see who we are by identifying who and what we value. Simply by taking time (which is not always easy) to think, remember and share we connect to that part of us that was given to us.

And it is something that was given to us.

To deny that people, places and events have shaped us is to turn away from our own place. It would be like the mountain denying the impact of the streams and waterfalls that shaped it, or the pot not recognizing the potter.

The search for our *Sense of Place* begins by seeing that place through the people and events that made us. There is that age-old question about whether leaders are made or born to lead. The answer is debatable, and probably both, but your place is definitely made for you.

Ho'omau—To Perpetuate
A *Sense of Place* is kind of like the tide—there are highs and lows. There are times when we feel full in the awareness of where we come from and other times where we are flat and listless.

Ho'omau means to continue, to keep something going, to preserve and keep constant. To continue in as full a *Sense of Place* as possible, to perpetuate and continue in this way of connection, there are activities and actions we can do.

Pictures
Picture albums, scrapbooks and slideshows are all excellent sources of place for us. When you have a camera (and many of us do all the time now with camera phones) take more pictures than you think you'll need. Rarely have I said "I wish I would have taken fewer pictures." Often have I said the opposite.

If you have pictures of your childhood somewhere, pull them out and go through them. If you have children of your own, show them your pictures and go through theirs regularly.

Stories

Tell stories about your life then tell them again. Tell them to your friends and family. Tell them so many times your kids will be able to tell them. Tell stories about the places you've been and people you've met. One of the reasons I'm against televisions in cars is that they take so much storytelling time away from families and give it to the DVD player. I'm OK with using them on extended car and air travel but, really, to the supermarket? Use the time you have to share and give and communicate.

As "advanced" as our society has become there is still room left for the oral tradition of passing down the mysteries and the histories of our families.

Also, listen to stories from your family and friends. One of the best ways to understand your own place is to hear about another's in their stories, people and events.

Travel

Another way to learn and know about your own place is to visit other places. There's something about travel that is expanding and even enlightening. A myopic, parochial viewpoint is not one usually associated with one well-travelled. You don't even have to travel far. Drive an hour or two in any direction and I bet you'll find a place you've never seen or experienced. Fly an hour or two (or many more) and for sure you'll find yourself recognizing elements of the place you come from in different, and if you're aware, deeper ways.

Genealogy

With the growth of online, searchable databases, researching and compiling your family tree has become remarkably more accessible. But you don't even have to own a computer to start. Go ask your parents or grandparents or an uncle or auntie about your family. Get them to start talking story with you about their story. Listen with more than your ears and your *Sense of Place* will grow more than you know.

The Oasis of Place
If your life is a trackless beach, then a *Sense of Place* is an oasis, a marker that always leads back to the core of who you are.

A deep *Sense of Place* keeps me respectful as I look to the future. Respectful means that I know there are shoulders I'm standing upon to reach higher, further and farther. I recognize the gifts I've received through the lives that have gone before and it keeps me humble.

Historically, when you heard "Somebody should put you back in your place!" it was meant as a demeaning and cutting remark. Now, I would love for someone to tell me that I know my place in the world. Without knowing that place it is difficult for us to stay grounded as we pursue our passions and purpose.

And being grounded and connected is a part of being and living *pono*.

HIGHLIGHTS

Place can be described as
- Our identity
- Roots
- An anchor
- Foundations

We understand where we are now by looking at the past in the same way that Hawaiian navigators track their current position out at sea.

Our past is often an accurate predictor of future "trends."

Our *Sense of Place* provides connection, confidence and a feeling of continuity within us and with the world around us.

Key people, events and places can help identify and ground us in our *Sense of Place*.

Emotional insecurities in our life are the identifiers of a weak *Sense of Place*. Find the things that make you insecure and you find the cracks in your foundation.

QUESTIONS

1. On a scale of 1-10, how strong is your *Sense of Place*?

2. What are the main stories in your life? Which ones do you tell over and over to your friends and family?

3. How has traveling to other places impacted your own *Sense of Place*?

4. Where are you most and least comfortable taking risks?

5. Who are/were the people that were most influential in your life and why?

6. Can you describe the things that make you feel insecure? Which are the biggest sources of fear?

KA‘ALA SOUZA

PART III: *PURPOSE*

'O ka makapō wale nō ka mea e hāpapa i ka pōuli
Only the blind gropes in the darkness.
"If you're going nowhere,
you're guaranteed to get there."
—Hawaiian Proverb

"The greatest danger for most of us is not that
our aim is too high and we miss it,
but that it is too low and we reach it."
—Michelangelo

"Don't ask yourself what the world needs;
ask yourself what makes you come alive.
And then go and do that. Because what the world
needs is people who have come alive."
—Howard Thurman

KAʻALA SOUZA

5
MOVING TO FOCUS

It's not daily increase but decrease. Hack away the unessential!—Bruce Lee

It's all fun and games until you get stuck.

We were out at a remote, 4x4 required, off-roading location just after midnight in my friend's truck. People were bouncing in the back, laughing it up and having a great time. Who knew that patch of sand on the beach would be so soft, treacherous and deep?

When we hit it we stopped, not abruptly, but slowly. We almost didn't recognize what was happening until we noticed how much slower and slower and s-l-o-w-e-r we were moving. Finally, we stopped altogether.

We kept on laughing it up—for about another five minutes. Then, when we finally realized, really realized, what "I think we're stuck" meant, the laughter all came to a stop, too.

The moon offered just enough light to scavenge for rocks, branches, trash—anything to provide traction to get out of the ever-deepening rut we were in. We kept piling things behind the wheels and the wheels kept turning and sinking deeper and deeper. We labored fruitlessly for over an hour before finally sending someone back for help.

We waited there another two hours before help arrived with a truck and a tow rope. Breakfast at McDonald's, as the sun rose over the mountains, never tasted so good.

Have you ever felt like that, like you were stuck in a rut? Maybe you've felt that for your whole life all you were doing was working to get a grip, to get enough traction to move just a little bit forward? Is your life's purpose dying in a 9-to-5 job and living for two days out of seven?

Purpose is to your life what caffeine is to your system.

I don't think so, and you probably don't either. Why is it then that this so brutally describes so many people that I've met? Why do so many not recognize the symptoms of a slowly sinking life until they're stuck way too deep for the rocks and branches of quick solutions?

A deep *Sense of Purpose* provides traction by providing the focus we need for our lives to move forward. Without focus our lives are tires spinning in the sand.

It follows that if a *Sense of Place* is where you come from then a *Sense of Purpose* is what you were made for and where you are going. Purpose is that thing that gets you up in the morning and injects the lifeblood into your day. Purpose is to your life what caffeine is to your system. If your life is *pono* then there is alignment between what you *think/feel/believe* and what you *do* on a day-to-day and minute-to-minute basis.

If your *Sense of Purpose* isn't clear you could spend your life scrambling, climbing, and crawling up the proverbial ladder, making it to the top— only then to realize the ladder was leaning against the wrong building!

It's why we see, hear and read about so many people who were "successful" in their businesses or careers but ended up depressed or despondent, discouraged, and in some cases, suicidal. We thought they "had it all" but obviously something was missing.

Before we get into the nuts and bolts and definitions let me share with you another story and some perspectives that hopefully can shed some light on what a *Sense of Purpose* means.

Did He Just Call Me a Jackass??

I had just left a meeting with my pastor where he started out by telling me how much potential I had and how much I could offer to the world around me. It made me feel good — until he added the always unexpected "but…" part. But, he said, something was missing.

He then went on to describe my life as unfocused and un-centered—like I was spinning my wheels in the sand, not applying myself and going nowhere. And this was a big enough "something" that, unless I addressed it, would severely limit my future.

Then he pulled out his bible, opened it to an obscure passage in Genesis and read

> "Issachar is a rawboned donkey
> lying down among the sheep pens.
> When he sees how good is his resting place
> and how pleasant is his land,
> he will bend his shoulder to the burden
> and submit to forced labor."

He closed the chapter, turned to me and said "This is you. You are doing and involved with so many things that, unless you're able to focus your gifts, your talents and your energies, this is the way your life will be. Do you want to live like this?"

Humph. Did he just call me a donkey? Did he just say I was a jackass? A wild, "rawboned" jackass? And did he just suggest that manual, "forced labor" was my future?

I admit I almost missed the point on this one for focusing on these other, less relevant questions. But still…

OK, at the time maybe I was a little overcommitted to maybe a lot of things. I was the head wrestling coach at a nearby high school, worked as a manager at a local surf shop, was going to college full-time and was the volunteer youth leader for a bunch of middle-school kids. I was involved with a lot of things, a lot of good things, in fact. There wasn't a problem with doing any of them, I wasn't dropping the ball anywhere, and these activities were all sailing along just fine, thank you.

And that was the problem. Everything was good, and nothing was great. My attention was so fragmented and my energy so splintered that what I was producing was coming out in pieces, with no focus, no center and no power. David Allen, a popular writer on personal productivity, says that "you can do anything, but not everything," and I was definitely trying to do everything.

There are so many things that tug and pull at us for our attention and energy. If we have no filter, no way to select and choose, then all the options are "good" ones. And if everything is good, really, in this case, nothing is good. If everything is a priority then nothing is a priority. Without something that tastes bad there's no way to measure what tastes good. There has to be a filter for us to judge between the two, make our choice and give 100 percent of ourselves to what we do, rather than offering up fragmented pieces of our attention and energy.

To this day, I'm not really sure what that bible verse really means, but for me, the pastor's words were a goad, a push to apply myself and "bend my shoulder to the labor."

I've never forgotten that meeting; it just took me many years before I could say I found my traction, my focus.

And no, I didn't want to then and still don't want to now —or ever—be a, uh, donkey. Thanks, Ralph.

Bruce Lee's One-Inch Power Punch

The power of focus. Did you ever burn a hole in a piece of paper or a leaf when you were a kid using your mom's magnifying glass, (who has one of those anymore?) out in the front yard, in the heat of the midday sun? I remember watching as I turned the glass a certain way, watching as the ray of light became more and more narrow, watching as a circle of smoke and charred edges began to form until finally my magnifying glass and I burned a satisfying hole in that leaf.

Ah, the good old days. Let there be fire!

The magnifying glass is the classic, very cliched but true, example of the power of focus.

Bruce Lee, the martial artist and movie star, had an incredible ability to channel and release energy in his kicks and punches. I saw a video demonstration of his "one-inch power punch," a punch he started one-inch away from the target. He hit a guy so hard that the man literally flew off his feet. The challenge of this punch was to develop enough momentum without the big windup to deliver a knock-out blow. His secret is no secret—it's focus.

When our actions are focused we move in a deliberate, set direction for a definite reason and objective. When my life's purpose is clear it becomes the magnifying glass for my sun. All of my energies are spent in conscious and determined effort for this purpose. I work and play, I live in tune with what I'm supposed to be doing.

When we possess this clarity of purpose there's no wasted motion. Living in this fashion we hold nothing back, there's no reserves and no regrets. All of that which is our person is centered on and targeted toward what we were created for. Our life becomes full and abundant. This is *pono*.

6
A SENSE OF PURPOSE IS...

A *Sense of Purpose*, then, is a sense of focus, of directed energy and intent. If place is the root then purpose is the trunk branching to the sky.

Purpose, in this sense, is the manifestation of what's important to you, of your values and principles, brought to life deliberately, on purpose. Strength of purpose is the extent to which you are conscious, aware and acting upon this manifestation.

With purpose there's wholeness. Without purpose we are shiftless, rootless, blown here, there and everywhere by any wind of whim or fancy, just like an absence of a *Sense of Place*. But in the case of purpose it's our actions rather than our identities that shift. We work on this project today and that one tomorrow, leaving most unfinished, unresolved and our own future uncertain. The connecting rungs are skipped, missed or forgotten all together until there's no way we're able to reach the top of the ladder.

Without a *Sense of Purpose* there's no connection to an overarching reason for what we do, think, behave or act. Any size fits all.

Have you seen those television commercials for medications that list all the possible, harmful side effects? Well, the symptoms in a life without a *Sense of Purpose* may include an unwillingness to wake up in the morning or a listlessness or lack of energy. Wake up? Me? Why? I'm going to be doing the same old thing, in the same old place for the same old people for the same old paycheck for the same old bills for the same old rent for the same old bed I'm laying in now. Why would this require me to be up and alert and engaged?

Symptoms may also include asking questions of yourself like, "Is this all there is?" or "Hey, this is not my beautiful house! How did I get here?" (to roughly paraphrase the music group, the "Talking Heads"). These questions reflect that part of us that recognizes we are not moving the way we were supposed to, we're getting deeper and deeper into the quicksand rut of an un-purposed life.

Unless what we do is deeply connected to our *Sense of Purpose*, we are constantly and continually spinning our lives in the sand, maybe moving, maybe even moving faster than the other trucks around us, but we're not going to be moving up to our potential, to where we should or could be.

We also won't be arriving anywhere close to the destination that is our life complete, full and abundant.

When we think of purpose there are two components that I believe should be included, certain complementary elements that should be a part of everyone's definition and direction. I don't usually prescribe so specifically; in fact, there are times I get in trouble because I'm too open to multiple viewpoints and perspectives. But, because of my own purpose, I feel I must. Even though you choose to disagree and reject these components, you would, at least, do it on purpose.

#1: Passion

My first prescription is passion. You should be passionate about your purpose in life. When you're talking about why you exist there should be, in a life of purpose, physiological evidence. Your pulse rate should increase, pupils dilate, and hands shake. You should be excited, leaning forward, with the pitch in your voice getting a little higher.

Maybe I'm getting a little metaphorical here but only a little. Someone listening to you describe the vision for your life's purpose should sense the passion. If there's nothing there in your description there's probably nothing there.

This is life to the fullest. When you're passion-focused life is totally, unequivocally w-o-r-t-h l-i-v-i-n-g! And why would you want to live in any other fashion? Who in the world would want to go through life flat, dull and boring? Who lives like this?

Well, only just most people.

When Thoreau writes that "most people lead lives of quiet desperation" this is what I believe he's talking about. They go to work, come home, go to work, come home again, rinse, repeat and do over ad infinitum and ad nauseum.

Like me and my friends getting stuck in the sand, they may not even know until it's too late and they're too deep to get out. There are no loud cries for help because there is no recognition of the desperateness of the situation, or even worse, because there is no hope for a solution.

Who Boils Frogs??
This is the classic case of the boiling frog. The idea there is that if you place a frog in a pot of boiling water it will immediately jump out. But if you place it in the pot when

the water is cold and gradually heat it, the frog will stay until boiled alive.

OK. Really?

First, let's ask who and why anyone would do this and then let's ask if it's true.

The answer to the first question, ruling out pathological frog haters, is a German physiologist from the 19th century who was studying, of all things, the location of our souls. He found that frogs with their brains removed would stay in a pot of slowly heated water but that whole-headed (?) frogs, with their brains all there, would attempt to jump out.

Uh, thanks for clearing that up. I would never have guessed.

A few other experiments with frogs and hot water continued on into the late 1800s. This led to quite a few folks, including former Vice-President Al Gore, quoting this strange behavior as a metaphor for people who were unaware and unresponsive to dangerous conditions around them.

When your brain is disconnected it makes for a dull and dreary existence.

In answer to the second question regarding its truthfulness, a quick skim of the internet will tell you probably not. But, it's still a terrific illustration of what we are looking at here: most people lead lives of quiet desperation, never recognizing, never comprehending, never acting no matter what happens to the temperature in the water around them.

When your brain is disconnected it makes for a dull and dreary existence.

A disconnected brain, in this case, is living without purpose. Having purpose with passion has the power to transform that gray, colorless life into a bright, vibrant mosaic of meaning.

The Intersection of Gladness and Hunger

I equate a *Sense of Purpose* with passion to the concept of calling. It's more than a career path or a job. Purpose and calling are better understood as a vocation. Something you do that is considered "very worthy" or requires great dedication would be a vocation. One dictionary definition also describes it as a "strong feeling of suitability."

The theologian Frederick Buerchner gives us two criteria for helping us discover our vocation and our purpose. He says this: "There are different kinds of voices calling you to different kinds of work, and the problem is to find out which is the voice of God rather than of Society say, or the Superego, or Self-Interest. By and large a good rule for finding out is this. The kind of work God usually calls you to do is work (a) that you need most to do and (b) that the world needs most to have done. The place God calls you to is the place where your deep gladness and the world's deep hunger meet."

The first time I read this I was completely blown away. What is it that I need "most to do" and that the world needs "most to have done?"

Most

There's an emphasis on priority with the word "most." In life there are many things we can do but not all of them are what we should do. When the menu of choices for our purpose is presented to us there's only one that is "most" suitable as a priority.

Deep

There's also an emphasis on meaning with the word "deep." When there is meaning in our life there is perseverance and determination. This depth contributes to our *Sense of Power* and perpetuity. Without this depth within, our purpose stalls and fades and we live the rest of our life in the doldrums. To quote Coleridge we are

> Day after day, day after day,
> We stuck, nor breath nor motion;
> As idle as a painted ship
> Upon a painted ocean.

When we combine our priorities, the "mosts" in our lives, with meaning, the "deep" in our lives, we have the conditions for finding the passion in our lives.

Wherever your purpose takes you, I submit that it will only be complete if it includes what you love, what excites you and what energizes you. I found this statement, attributed to Howard Thurman, that puts passion in the right place in finding our *Sense of Purpose*:

> *Don't ask yourself what the world needs; ask yourself what makes you come alive. And then go and do that. Because what the world needs is people who have come alive.*

#2: Kākou-Focused

"Consciously or unconsciously, every one of us does render some service or other. If we cultivate the habit of doing this service deliberately, our desire for service will steadily grow stronger, and will make, not only our own happiness, but that of the world at large."—Mahatma Gandhi

There are two words in Hawaiian that can describe a group of us—*kākou* and *mākou*. Both technically mean "we" or "us" whenever there are more than three people together. They differ in that *mākou* is exclusive, that is, just our group and no one else. I've often heard someone give a greeting to a group with the phrase "*Aloha kākou!* Let there be *aloha* between all of us." I've only once ever heard someone say "*Aloha mākou,*" meaning that the *aloha* we have is only for a select group of us and no one else. This happened in a contentious public forum that, frankly, shocked me in it's un-*aloha*ness. I mean, be mad, be upset, but never be un-aloha.

The heart, the essence of *aloha* is always inclusive, it's always *kākou*. Our *Sense of Purpose* needs to be, as well.

The second part of my prescription is an *all of us*-orientation. By that I mean an awareness that our existence should contribute to improving the existence of others. With this viewpoint, a mindset of what's-in-it-for-me? instead becomes a worldview of what's-in-it-for-us?

This can be hard. Why should we care about someone else's problems when I have so many of my own?

I can answer simply that it's the right thing to do, it's *pono*.

People can say that right and wrong are relative and my right is not for them and who am I, anyway, to define what's right and wrong?

I can say true to that. If someone considers carefully and arrives at the conclusion that in their purpose on this planet there is no need for being conscious of and serving the needs of others around them, then, though I disagree, I can respect that deliberate decision.

If, on the other hand, you disregard this idea of interdependence and service, almost casually by your lack of considering the topic, I believe you do yourself a disservice.

Maturity is understanding our mutual need for one another, our interdependence.

When my children were younger they were completely dependent upon us as parents for everything. We fed them, bathed them, burped them and, ahem, changed them. We gave them everything. As they grew older they became more independent, as they should, doing things for themselves and on their own. As they mature we are moving into a relationship of mutual interdependence, where we give and we receive and they give and they receive.

A lack of this recognition, basically an overly dependent or independent frame of mind, limits our own development and our potential growth. So, maybe, including giving and serving in our purpose lifestyle is somewhat selfish. I can live with that. Ralph Waldo Emerson said it like this:

It is one of the most beautiful compensations of life, that no man can sincerely try to help another without helping himself.

Including the concept of service in our purpose is win-win and it's a *pono* thing.

7
PURPOSEFUL DISCOVERY

Now the question is how do we chart our course to discover this passion and service? Does it just—happen? If I go about my business in this world will I effortlessly fall upon the fullness of my *Sense of Purpose* like a serendipitous find at a weekend garage sale? Whew. Maybe. I think for some, it's yes they do, for whatever reason, fall into their life's purpose naturally, or maybe even accidentally. For the rest of us the return comes with more investment in effort, deliberation and activity.

For some it's trial and error; for others, sadly, in error, they don't even try.

The Polynesian Voyaging Society (PVS) was formed in 1973 with a major goal to build and sail a traditional Polynesian canoe to demonstrate that purposeful and deliberate long-distance ocean voyaging between islands was possible.

One of the standard schools of thought in those days was that the majority of the islands in the Pacific were settled accidentally by islanders blown off course by a storm while at sea fishing. Some anthropologists believed that the islands could not have have been settled any other way because the required navigation tools and deep-sea worthy vessels were not available.

The first canoe they built, named *Hōkūleʻa*, meaning "Star of Gladness," was constructed to demonstrate that the Pacific Islanders had the skills and wherewithal to travel thousands of miles across the largest body of water in the world and populate its island groups on purpose.

In 1976, the *Hōkūleʻa* set sail from Oʻahu, Hawaiʻi, against the prevailing winds, against the prevailing Humboldt current, and against the prevailing mindset at the time. They made landfall a month later in Tahiti demonstrating a wayfinding approach that far exceeded all expectations.

Understand that navigating the Pacific and charting a course for our lives are two, very similar, very parallel engagements. What may look like endless miles of trackless ocean actually contains, for those who know where and how to look, "landmarks," or more appropriately, "oceanmarks," suitable for finding your way on the journey.

Wayfinding on the seemingly trackless expanse of life requires similar skills and knowledge. You have to know where to look and how to see the lifemarks in front of you.

And, you have to do it purposefully.

You'll See it When You Know it

When you're living and working in this *Sense of Purpose* you'll know it.

Time seems to fly unnoticed, you feel excited, challenged, energized, alive and focused. It's a part of how I understand Mihaly Csíkszentmihályi's concept of Flow, that mental state of being where a person is fully engaged, immersed and involved with the process of an activity. Csíkszentmihályi says that when you're in this state of flow you have feelings of "spontaneous joy, even rapture, while performing a task."

When we expand this to include the combined tasks of all that we do, at home and at work, we are then living in *Sense of Purpose*.

There's research out there that suggests our minds can only pay attention to a limited amount of information at a time. This is why multitasking, once thought to be a skill to highlight at job interviews, is coming under fire. According to one study, our brains can handle about 126 bits of information per second. To put this into perspective, a normal conversation requires about 40 bits per second, making watching the football game on television, reading the paper and having a meaningful conversation with your spouse challenging.

> **If everything is important in your life, nothing is important.**

I don't know how accurate the research is but I do know that in my life there have been times when I've been not only multitasking but multipurposing.

If you know that trying to make everyone happy is not going to cut it, try following multiple purposes for yourself. It'll drive you crazy or lazy. You'll either go nuts or stop doing anything worthwhile because you're overloaded with important things. If everything is important in your life, nothing is important.

The research from Csíkszentmihályi tells us that clear goals and direction along with immediate feedback and confidence in one's ability to perform a task promotes flow.

Similarly, there are certain conditions within us that must be met before a *Sense of Purpose* is manifested. They revolve around a clear understanding of self and what you means.

When you're clear on your YOU you'll know it, and when you know it, well, that's when you'll see it.

Death As a Guest Lecturer

I found my *you*, the me that is truly me, the hard way. In one twelve-month period I was faced with different aspects of death that made me rethink the rest of my life. There were things I saw that year, now over a decade ago, that brought into focus what was truly important to and as me.

Thinking about death is sort of a morbid way to approach life. It may be a little gruesome at first but there's little doubting death's power to highlight meaning and purpose in our lives. Who on their deathbed ever wished to clean and organize their cubicle one last time? Who has hoped that their last breath could be drawn in just one more conference room meeting?

I'd rather you not have to suffer through the near-death experiences so will share mine in the hope that it offers you motivation to look and see now rather than later.

Death is a very motivating guest lecturer.

Wrong Turn

It was an almost fatal wrong turn.

My wife and I were returning from a meeting in an unfamiliar place on a dark and winding road. It was late in the night as we headed back to stay overnight with her parents.

I thought we were on a state highway when we came upon a road sign that highways are not supposed to have. The sign, like an upside down letter "L" indicated a sharp right hand turn and a speed limit of 15 mph. No highway this! I had somehow gotten turned around and ended up on a rural, residential back road!

I immediately pumped the brakes, attempting to navigate the turn, knowing as I did that we were going way too fast. There was a ditch and pasture in front of us that I angled the rental car into, still trying to slow down as we shot into the field.

We must've been airborne at least once when we left the road. Somehow, in the split seconds all this was happening I felt my wife's hand in mine and heard her saying "I love you, Kaala." Time really felt as though it stood still. This could only have taken a handful of seconds, bare moments in time, yet it felt like forever.

Abruptly, still holding hands and whispering to each other, the front end of our car rammed into a concrete wall. The field had slowed us down sufficiently to keep the airbags from deploying but the collision was still strong enough to leave an impact for many months to come (my wife had neck problems for several years after); it left a much more lasting imprint on my soul.

This may sound obvious but I recognized at that point the importance of my family. It wasn't as though I were derelict or absent before the accident, but somehow this event cemented the primacy of my wife and my children in my purpose.

Shortly after this incident we made some pretty drastic changes. I left my job in a wonderful marketing research company to have more time with my family. We decided to homeschool our children and that I would start my own company doing training and consulting that I could operate from home.

It made for some difficult financial times in the early years but it was the right thing, the *pono* thing for us to do.

Cancer Bucket List

I was one of those people who had never wondered what I would do if I were told I only had six months to live. I was forced to address that ignorance after leaving the doctor's office on a sunny, but somehow gloomy, day.

My doctor's office was just around the block from my house so I had walked over, enjoying the sunshine, for my appointment to hear the results of a biopsy performed a couple of weeks prior. I remember walking in, talking to the doctor, asking him to repeat what he said, asking him to write it down, then leaving. Outside the office, in a mental fog, I clutched the scrap piece of paper with the word malignant scrawled next to some scientific-sounding cancer type.

I wasn't sure what to think or how to act.

My wife, a intensive-care nurse, was at work and I couldn't contact her until later.

I got home (somehow), sat at my desk and typed the doctor's description in my internet search bar and tried to figure out what was going on. A whole bunch of pages with my type of cancer returned with my search query. I couldn't understand the terminology of the diagnosis.

I sat and I waited and I thought.

When my wife came home later that evening I handed her the slip of paper. She looked at my search results and quietly researched the cancer. Then she began to cry.

As she was able she explained the type of cancer I had and what we could expect; it wasn't looking good. She called her mother, also a nurse, and explained the situation. They were both crying on the phone. I heard them making plans for my mother-in-law to come and help with our children.

I don't remember telling our kids what was happening but we must have. My youngest was too young to fully understand but I remember him praying for me.

Over the next couple of weeks we eventually told some of our close friends and family members.

My wife and I spent a lot of time together, thinking and talking and working hard at trying to glue back the shattered pieces of our life and what we had envisioned for our future.

When I was alone I did what I did upon first hearing the news—I sat and waited and thought. I remember making a list, people call it a bucket list now, of what I wanted to do in the time I had left.

The first thing on the list was to re-read Anne of Green Gables out loud with our children. I always read to them, or told them made-up stories, at night before bedtime and this was one of our all-time favorites.

Another thing on my list was to kayak the beautiful and mysterious Na Pali coast on the island of Kaua'i, spending time exploring and camping on the way.

Finally, I remember wanting to use whatever remained of my life to make a difference for other people, to contribute in a way that lasted and endured.

Again, what was important in my life was brought into sharp focus and alignment. Through a touch of the void, of the great beyond, my values in this life were being shaped into something starting to look *pono*.

It took a face-to-face with death to initiate an about face in my life.

It took a face-to-face with death to initiate an about face in my life. The subsequent life decisions and choices I made have all been influenced by that meeting.

These death encounters provided some shock therapy clarity for my purpose by showing me the love of my family, the need for me to make a lasting difference and the requirement for me to share what I have. These events clarified the me to me.

To make a long story short, I don't have that cancer. People ask me what happened and I can only shrug. About a month after we first found out, my oncologist and his partner after rechecking and even sending the biopsy off to Harvard met with my wife and me, telling us, and I quote:

"We looked and we've changed our mind. We don't see the cancer any longer."

I don't know what happened or what they saw first and didn't see after. All I know is that my family and my church were praying for me and for one very long month I lived as though I were dying. That month changed the rest of my life. It was like years of uncertainty were being chiseled off me. What was fuzzy became more clear. An outline of my reason for being, my purpose, was starting to show in the sculpture of my life.

Who are You and What are You Doing Here?

There's a story told of a research scientist working in Europe during WWII. It was late at night and he couldn't sleep so had wandered out of the special section set apart for his team and into a restricted area.

Suddenly, a harsh, bright spotlight blinded him and he heard a commanding voice bark out, "Halt! Who are you and what are you doing here?"

Stunned by the light and the intensity of the soldier, the scientist was still able to realize the depth and importance of the questions. He replied, "I will pay your salary and give you room and board if every day you will ask me those selfsame two questions!"

These two questions are some of the most important anyone can ask you. Who are you and what are you doing here? Can you answer them? Not on the simplistic levels of "My name is ___" and "I'm taking a walk," but on a more meaningful plane that drills down deeper into the core of the who and what in your life.

If having a strong *Sense of Place* shows who and where we come from, purpose directs where we go. The place question of "who" provides answers of priorities and values in that direction while the purpose question of "what" gives us answers of meaning in our actions. These two things are what we need to be *pono* in our lives. No one can answer them for us.

Though all are given the same questions, the results will be unique to each of us.

This is where we can say that we are *pono*—when our values, our who, and our actions, our what, are in alignment, in harmony, in rightness.

The *Pono* Q&As
The following questions can take you five minutes or five hours to answer—I would do both. Get your journal or notepad and jot down your immediate responses to the questions. Don't worry about spelling, punctuation and the like—just write. Then over the next week or so, revisit, think, rewrite, think and write some more.

If you haven't done something like this before it may seem either too easy or too difficult. Stay with it. I assure you the rewards are worth the effort.

Follow Your Passions, Find Your Purpose
Where your strengths intersect with your passion there you will find vocation, calling and purpose. It is not enough to be passionate about starting a business, you must have certain character traits, skills and strengths. You won't be getting a PGA golf pro card just because you really, really care about golfing.

Take some time and work through the following questions and see what happens. After you've listed down your responses, or if you get stuck, ask someone you trust and who cares about you enough to tell you the truth, to review the questions and your answers and to give you their feedback. Again, you'll see the need to look backwards to be able to move forwards. Your *Sense of Place* is a strong contributor to your *Sense of Purpose*.

Here are the first questions:

1. What are you good at? Really. Don't just think about those job-interview type answers like "I can multitask" or "I'm a team player" and move on. Are you really good at them? What are your strengths? What are your weaknesses?

2. Where have you been successful in the past?

3. When you think about satisfying projects you have participated in, completed or delivered, which ones come to mind?

4. What activities have you done that made you feel like you were in the flow, in the zone while doing them?

Another way to look at this is to ask which activities when you finished, left you feeling energized and pumped rather than exhausted and tired? A lot of people have to give presentations and talks at work or community groups. Many of them finish and leave exhausted. Public speaking, while an activity all can learn, is not something all leave feeling refreshed and revitalized. I do, and other speakers I know do as well. In the same way, identify your energizers and de-energizers then continue on through the rest of the questions in this section.

If Failure is Impossible?

"Some men see things as they are and say, Why? I of dream things that never were, and say, Why not?" —George Bernard Shaw

Two words: why and not. Put together they can stop you or propel you. Some would look at those two words as stoppers and be able to give you such a grand canyon of "nots" that no one would ever be able to cross it. Others, and this is where we want to be, will look at "why not" and be inexorably and irresistibly pulled forward towards their dreams.

What would you do if you knew you couldn't fail?

Think about it. The world is your oyster (if you like oysters). What would you do? Start a business? Go to school? Change careers? Climb Mt. Everest? Write down the ideas that come to mind in your journal without passing judgment on yourself (i.e. without all the "nots"!).

Continue by adding another thing (or things) you would do or achieve. For example, if all your college expenses were paid for what would study and why? If expenses were not an issue what would you spend your life doing?

It was Lewis Mumford who said, "The cities and mansions that people dream of are those in which they finally live." Basically, the house your body lives in starts in your brain. Give yourself the freedom to dream and dream big.

If Money is No Concern?

Sometimes our passions and purposes are limited by our own rationality. We say "It would cost too much," or "I have a day job," or any number of reasonable and practical financially-orientated objections. Stop. For now. Take your mind off the limitations imposed by your built-in accountant and ask yourself:

What would I spend my life doing if money were no concern?

If you didn't have to work to pay bills and get by, what would you do? What would you spend your time engaged in?

Eulogy Analysis

One of the most effective tools for helping you to get deep into meaning, priorities and values is what I call the Eulogy Analysis. I first read about this years ago in a book from Stephen Covey.

The question is simple:

What would you want people to say about you at your funeral?

First, make a list of the major roles you have and the people they represent. I personally include my roles as husband (my wife), dad (my children), family member (my extended family), pastor (my church), business owner (my clients), friend (my friends), and community member (the world around me). You should have, roughly, six to eight main responsibilities on your list.

Second, and this is the key to the whole exercise, you must describe what you would want them to say if you lived that role in the best, most excellent way possible. In other words, if you were the best parent, the best spouse, the best manager you could possibly be, what would those people say about you?

The more you do this the deeper you go. The deeper you go the more *pono* you become.

Joy Unlimited

There is no one-size-fits-all purpose. Your purpose really fits only you.

Your answers to the questions in this section get your canoe started in the generally right direction. As you travel there are constant, mostly minor, course corrections. That's

OK for me and *pono*. The key thing is to get your canoe moving. In fact, you can only steer when your canoe is moving.

Our *Sense of Place*, if in place, provides a starting point, a home base to launch from and search for our *Sense of Purpose*.

And search we must. Left to its own device, our purpose is elusive and secretive. Sure some may stumble upon theirs, but most will have to work for it as though digging for gold or buried treasure. Still others, sadly, will go through their entire lives never even realizing that they *should be* looking.

Consider these two search and find descriptions relating to an ultimate purpose from a master teacher:

"The kingdom of heaven is like treasure hidden in a field. When a man found it, he hid it again, and then in his joy went and sold all he had and bought that field."

"Again, the kingdom of heaven is like a merchant looking for fine pearls. When he found one of great value, he went away and sold everything he had and bought it."

If you seek your purpose you will find it, and when you find it your joy will be limitless.

HIGHLIGHTS

Purpose is to your destination as Place is to your identity.

A *Sense of Purpose* provides:

- Traction
- Priorities
- Focus
- Intention
- Reason

In our Purpose we find the manifestation of the important in our life. Purpose answers the question of what our principles, values and priorities are in life.

A strong *Sense of Purpose* is the answer to the problem of weak finishing skills by providing reasons for what we do, why we think a certain way and how we behave.

Purpose without passion leads to a flat, colorless existence.

Purpose without service to others is a dis-service to yourself.

Finding your *Sense of Purpose* and traditional Polynesian wayfinding are similar when we utilize "oceanmarks" and "lifemarks" deliberately to chart our course.

Living on Purpose contributes to Flow, being fully engaged and energized for life at home and work.

QUESTIONS

1. On a scale of 1-10, how strong is your *Sense of Purpose*?

2. Have you ever felt like the frog boiling alive or like Thoreau's "quietly desperate"?

3. When have you experienced being in the state of Flow?

4. What makes you come alive?

PART IV: *POWER*

He pukoʻa kani ʻāina
A coral reef that grows into an island.
"A person beginning in a small way gains steadily
until he becomes firmly established."
—Hawaiian Proverb

You don't have a soul.
You are a Soul.
You have a body.
—C. S. Lewis

KAʻALA SOUZA

8
HURRICANES AND FLAT SURF

We were looking forward to the storm; there was a hurricane coming and we actually welcomed it. The hurricane itself was far out to sea and not likely to hit, but it brought the chance for large surf to our normally surf-less shore. After loading up our boards and gear in the truck we headed for the beach.

We usually walked but that day we sprinted down the narrow, sandy trail.

As we got closer and closer our running got slower and slower—not because we were out of breath (well, maybe a little bit) but mostly because it was so still and quiet.

Where was the sound of the crashing surf, the waves pounding on the sand? Where was the sea mist spray, the salty tang in the air?

We looked for surf but found... flat. What a drag.

As the path opened up and we caught our first view of the ocean, we saw that the view was all we would catch that morning. It was flat. Totally. Not a ripple, not a wave. Big Monday wasn't going to happen. It was picturesque, true, but there was nothing surf-able, nothing to move us. For some reason the projected high surf had missed our section of the island.

Bummer, dude, bummer.

And this, for some, is what life looks like daily.

All around them is a 360° view of flatness. They sit in this unmoving ocean of their lives, passionless, powerless, unable to generate enough energy to lift off the proverbial couch. There is no current and no pull in any direction. No drive, no push, no movement. It's flat like a half-empty can of cola left open and unfinished for too long.

We all start out eager and excited, dreamers dreaming the big dream, but not all finish this way. We hustle about getting ready, preparing ourselves, sprinting down the path, only to find that the big swell passed us by, or never showed up, or we were in the wrong place at the wrong time, or that person didn't do what they promised, or…the list of why and how and what we missed is endless and pointless.

We've been dragged down over and over and don't want to get up any more.

I've known the haves and have-nots and neither is immune from the drag of flat. Flatness doesn't have anything to do with rich or poor, middle, lower or upper-class. It's not confined to a specific location or population. I'd wager that we have all succumbed, to one degree or another, to this negative pull.

Flat is manifested in our attitudes and our health. It affects our performance at work and our relationships at home, often playing on one at the expense of the other.

Look around and you'll see the evidence of flat all around and in us. To counter this always present poison the antidote needs to be everywhere with us as well.

9
A SENSE OF POWER IS...

A *Sense of Power* is the push against the pull of flat. This power moves and sustains us. It's our inspiration, our motivation and perpetuating energy. This feeling enables us to continue. It both produces and is the outcome of peak happiness and health.

Our *Sense of Power* is, of course, deeply dependent and related to our *Sense of Place* and *Purpose*. If *Place* and *Power* start us moving, then we finish through this *Sense of Power*.

The purpose is our destination, the power is our fuel along the way.

> Without a *Sense of Place* it's hard to know where you are.
>
> Without a *Sense of Purpose* you won't know where you're going.
>
> Without a *Sense of Power* you won't have a chance of getting there.

Our power base is drawn from our past and our present, our internals and externals. People and experiences have contributed, sometimes without us even aware, to who we are. A strong connection to our place in this world produces a strong motivation to continue and extend the world.

Even negative past inputs can be recycled as positives.

A little over ten years ago, at the end of a presentation on this topic, a lady came up to me in tears. She described her positive motivation to be a loving mother, to protect and provide for her children, as coming from just the opposite in her own upbringing. She desperately wanted her children to have the love she never had. That absence produced a power-full incentive to live her life differently.

All three aspects of *pono*—place, purpose and power—are identifiably separate on paper, but often indistinguishable in practice.

Of the three, this *Sense of Power*, even though it's a topic I've spent over twenty-five years studying, researching and trying to apply in my life, is arguably the most difficult for me to define.

This difficulty is most likely due to the duality and often apparent contradictions inherent in how I think of it.

Power is at times both

- Self-controlled and uncontrollable
- Internal and external
- Produced in me and absorbed by that around me
- Simultaneously present and future
- Focused and disciplined as well as wild and untamed.

Power also has different meanings and connotations for each of us. Some hear the word power and think of the physical—things like cars, engines, sports, lifting, running, throwing, jumping. Others will hear it and think of control, of corporations, moving up the ladder, money and mergers. Still others may think of that which is natural—the ocean, mountains, avalanches, earthquakes and tsunamis. All these are certainly what it means.

One thing that I can't avoid in my life is the implied spirituality in a *Sense of Power*.

Sense of the Spiritual

Occasionally, and it adds some spice here, people may associate power with the spiritual, the unseen, the unknowable and unsearchable. When when we talk about the spiritual in this fashion we talk about religions and non-religions, faiths and beliefs, the unnatural and supernatural.

As we move into this area we are faced with not just the intellectual but the emotional. Religion is, after all, one of those topics, along with politics, that we don't discuss at parties.

But, when I say spiritual do I mean religious? Yes and no. Let me explain.

This sense of the spiritual is, almost by exclusion, all that is not physical, mental, or emotional for me. It is a connection with something that is beyond, greatly beyond who and what I am.

The spiritual is about faith, though not always a man-made one. For some this translates into a particular religion, structured or otherwise. This "religion" is defined as a set of beliefs that dictates worldview, the why and how our universe (including our own self) came to be, acts and behaves.

When I think religion I generally include the world's major belief sets; for example, Islam, Christianity, Buddhism, Hinduism, etc.

For others, what they believe may be less systematic, though, in my mind, not any less religious by the above definition. It is more of a feeling or an awareness, maybe a more intuitive interaction with the world around them.

Maybe you've noticed in this section (in fact, even in this sentence!) a lot more "mays" and "maybes" looseness in describing religion, systematic or otherwise, than anywhere else in this book. A topic like this is probably (there's that looseness again!) easier to describe than to define.

Religion can also be loosely defined as your set of beliefs about the "cause, nature and purpose of the universe." With this definition you would be religious if you believe God created the world in seven days or that there is no "creator" and the world evolved over billions of years.

Religion doesn't have to be a "bad" word. When someone cuts you off on the freeway or you hit your thumb with a hammer you don't have to use "religion" as your expletive. It can certainly be either positive or negative.

I believe (my worldview) that you can be spiritual—and in fact to be *pono* you must be—without belonging to an identifiable religion. I also believe that you can be non-spiritual at the same time that you do belong to a religion. Ouch. In fact, I've spent most of my life in an identifiable religion, working as a pastor to help people, wherever they were at, move into the spiritual, beyond just the motions or rituals.

The challenge to be *pono* remains the same whether we believe in a personal God or not. We must have a connection to this intangible or we are incomplete and out of alignment.

When there is access to a strong power base our purpose has the potential to be fully realized. Without it, we flounder, we squander, we miss and fall short of the target that is the full and complete life.

How do we know if there is a strong *Sense of Power* in our lives? The presence or absence of this kind of strength is distinguished by two things that we can use as measures, as power gauges if you will. These two things are happiness and strength. They're "simple complex" indicators, meaning that they are at once both simple to understand and sometimes impossibly complex!

Once we break down the definitional complexity we are faced with a pretty straightforward evaluation.

We'll start with happy.

KAʻALA SOUZA

10
HAPPY HAPPENS

Happy is underrated! Why is it that the idea of personal happiness, of wanting to be happy, is somehow a bad thing or selfish? Isn't that in the Declaration of Independence or something?

The pursuit of happiness is something that more and more people seem to consider alien rather than an inalienable right.

Ultimately, happy happens when who we are, what we do and how we do are in alignment. Happy happens when we are *pono* and *pono* happens when we are happy. They follow and lead after each other. This is a good thing.

There's an old Hawaiian proverb that states:

> *Hahai no ka ua i ka ulula'au.*
> The rain follows after the forest.

When I first read this I was confused; isn't it the other way around? Isn't the forest supposed to follow after the rain? It makes sense to me that if I watered my garden it grew. This seemed backwards.

Luckily for the ancients, they had a deeper understanding of cause and effect. The lush forests of Hawai'i act as "cloud nets," almost drawing the rain towards them. The roots of the trees and surrounding plants would absorb, protect and channel the water productively. Cut down the trees, take away the forest, and you change the entire system.

The interdependent relationship of the rain to the trees and plants is a wonderful example of *pono* and happiness. In the long run it doesn't matter which comes first. When I'm living in true happiness I'm *pono*. When I'm *pono* I'm happy.

Happy Test
I enjoy tests that tell me something about me or my personality. If the results are good I agree and speak well of the test designers. Of course, if I strongly disagree with the results, the test and the designers were dead wrong. Just kidding.

Here's a fun, simple test to check your happiness levels. Ready?

Are you happy?

That's it. Simple question, yes or no. Did you expect more?

With this "test" you can tell a lot about yourself. Your answer, along with how you answered, is revealing.

If you answered quickly with a affirmative or negative you would seem to have a clear understanding of happy as a concept. You have a definition and you know where you're at. It's not even required that your understanding be the same as anyone else's.

If it was harder for you to come up with an answer maybe the problem was trying to define the word happy.

It's always more difficult to answer yes/no when you're unsure of the measures and meaning. Being uncertain of what happy means should tell you something. If I don't know whether I'm happy or not I should know that I'm confused about my place and purpose. It's going to be very difficult for me to find a sense of sustaining power without an understanding of happiness.

Another possible way this shows up and you could have answered is to have asked your own counterquestion—what is happiness—and safely not answered the question. Because, wait, isn't happy one of those words that each of us interprets differently? This is a sleight of hand denial technique.

And while I agree that the word is ambiguous with meaning determined by personal perceptions, this way of answering still smacks of confusion and high level confusion leads to low power production.

So, let me try and clarify my understanding of happy by flipping it over and looking at what is not happy. This kind of backwards approach might be able to help us come up with a happy definition.

What Happy is NOT

Happy, is not some giddy, sky-high, up in the stratosphere kind of feeling.

Happiness, and for sure the idea of joy, is a deeper running current, sometimes different from the surface direction. In other words, my circumstances and surroundings might be down and negative but deep inside I can still remain buoyant and positive.

Happiness can coexist with difficult circumstances. When I'm euphoric I'm definitely happy but the opposite isn't always true. I can be challenged and in difficult, non-euphoric producing circumstances and still be happy.

This reminds me of a powerful verse from the bible:

Consider it pure joy, my brothers and sisters, whenever you face trials of many kinds, because you know that the testing of your faith produces perseverance.

Being happy in spite of our circumstances is a depth test for joy.

Some would say that the ideas of peace, or contentment or well-being would better communicate this and it very well could be. If I expand my understanding from an overly simplistic "happy meal" mindset to a broader sense of positive, the word happy will work for what I'm looking for.

> **Being happy in spite of our circumstances is a depth test for joy.**

Let's say, for the sake of discussion, that happy is a general feeling of positive, of good, of right, of smiles, of satisfaction, of well-being; that sounds like happy to me.

When looking at the opposite—the negative, the bad, the wrong, the frowns and frustration—I think we're pretty clear on what not happy is so let's flip it, take the negative of that negative, and get not-not happy and call that happy.

I'm confused just reading that paragraph. How about you simply answer the question:

Are you happy?

11
C'MON GET HAPPY!!

Way, way back in the day one of the most popular television shows around was the Partridge Family. ABC's Friday night show told the story of a mom and her five kids as they traveled around in their brightly colored bus singing and guess what, yep, making people happy.

I remember Shirley Jones, David Cassidy and Danny Bonaduce (who I don't think was really playing or singing anything) and their theme song, "C'mon Get Happy!" The theme sings of the "whole lot of lovin'" they bring everywhere they travel. C'mon get happy! Shucks, I'm singing it even now.

(Warning: if you know it and start singing along right now, it will be stuck in your head for the rest of the day! Sorry...)

It was catchy and upbeat and every time I think about "how to get happy" I can't help but hum the tune.

Six Getting Happy Principles

There is debate about whether or not one can just "get happy" but not too much argument from the research suggesting that the happier you are the better. Duh. It sounds like a no-brainer but it goes deeper than just a little "better" since happy people tend to live longer and more fulfilling lives.

Isn't that what we're looking for here? Did we just find the secret fountain of youth?

I've read a couple of studies that suggest that the size of our happiness "tank" is set and finite. You can work on keeping it filled but there's not much you can do to increase the capacity. This means that your max happiness score is fixed and as unchangeable as your height.

I wouldn't worry too much about this since most people I meet haven't even come close to limiting out their quota and have lots of room left in their happy tank.

What we should be working on are the things that fill that tank. I'm going to share a list of activities that have worked for me and many others. Your mileage may vary. The key is to experiment and try things and evaluate the results.

Don't get all negative if you see something that looks dumb or silly (especially if you haven't tried it).

In fact, recognize that if something makes you uncomfortable it may be something that you should move towards rather than away from. If your current level of happiness is low and you argue with something you haven't tried, well…

Give it a shot and then grumble if it doesn't work.

1. You have to want it.

Before anything else you have to accept that being happy is not only OK but it's something you want. I'm not sure where we went astray on this one but even Oprah talks about this. And if Oprah is talking about it, it must be important. :)

2. Live Pono.

Yeah, I'm not sure if I can put this in the book on living *pono* without being accused of circular reasoning but I firmly believe that if you're not living from a strong *Sense of Place, Purpose* and *Power* you won't be happy. I mentioned it earlier but it bears repeating: happiness follows *pono* and *pono* follows happiness. Work on the things that will bring strong alignment in your life and you will find you won't have to go looking for happiness, it'll already have found you.

If you're living on purpose it means you're living for a reason and there's meaning in your life. All the studies I'm reading suggest that without this your chances of happiness are drastically reduced.

And don't make the mistake of thinking that "if only" I had more money or more of that or this thing that you'd be happier. Money, possessions or other extrinsics you put on the outside will only get you so far; the brunt of the happiness platform is built on what you can get inside of you.

3. Think about the "right" things.

A scripture from the Bible says

Finally, brothers and sisters, whatever is true, whatever is noble, whatever is right, whatever is pure, whatever is lovely, whatever is admirable—if anything is excellent or praiseworthy—think about such things.

If your brain is thinking about the above list it won't have time to think about the negatives. Where your brain goes the energy flows. Your life follows your energy.

4. Stop pursuing happiness.

Henry David Thoreau says "Happiness is like a butterfly: the more you chase it, the more it will elude you, but if you turn your attention to other things, it will come and sit softly on your shoulder."

The concept here is that the more we push for this ethereal sense of happiness, the more we make it our direction and desire, the more difficult it will be to achieve. This is why I stress working on aligning the things we've been talking about in this book and letting the happiness follow. Stop looking for happiness and start looking for your *Sense of Place*, *Purpose* and *Power*.

5. Start pursuing happiness.

This at first (and probably second) glance looks like something of a contradiction of the previous injunction to "stop looking for happiness" and it kind of is. Sorry. The thing is I believe we find what we're looking for and I'm wanting to find happiness. Why would I pretend I'm not? I'm not dumb and neither are you. Even if we say you won't find happiness by looking at it directly and I have to come at it from a different angle I'll still know that I'm still looking for happiness. So, I'm supposed to trick myself? And I'll fall for this? Yes. And this is OK. Make every effort to find happiness. If it's good enough to put in the United States' Declaration of Independence it's good enough for me.

6. Be here, not there.

This is the Principle of Presence, of being in the moment, in the now. Wherever and whenever you are, be THERE. When you're on vacation sitting on that lovely white sand Hawaiian beach don't be thinking about the report that's due when you get back or the yard work piling up at home. Be there fully and completely.

One of the worst (from a life-balance/*pono* perspective) advertisements I've ever seen was a poster hung in a window at a local gas station. It was a wireless broadband company demonstrating its product. The picture showed a guy sitting at the beach on a lounge chair with his computer on his lap watching his kids playing, swimming and making sand castles.

Really?

Seriously, I can't think of a better illustration of the absence of this principle.

Each moment we have is one we won't have again; savor it. Taste it. Appreciate it. Live it fully.

And speaking of living it, now that we've gone over the principles let's get to some of the "practicals."

Happy is a Skill

Happy is something you are and something you do. If the latter is true, you can do more happy and if you do more you can improve. Happy is a skill and remember that old adage about "practice makes perfect?" Well, practicing the activities below makes happy.

Remember, if something strikes you as weird or dumb or useless and you haven't experimented with it yet, don't write it off. Give it at least a week or two—even better, a month— before you move on.

Also, what's practical for some may not be for you. Examine your life circumstance and if it's truly impossible or difficult to implement some of these ideas then modify or shelve them for later.

1. Sleep

Think about it. Do you get more crabby and grumpy when you're sleep deprived? This is one simple and (relatively) easy thing you can do that will yield enormous benefits. Experiment with this for thirty days. Work on going to sleep and waking up close to the same time every day, workday or weekend, shooting for seven to eight hours of sleep a night (or whatever number you've found wakes you up energized and alert). A perfect sleep is when I wake up with no outside help—no alarm ringing, message texting, birds chirping, bathroom calling, hunger demanding—just my body naturally rising after rest.

Don't stop after three days because you feel sluggish or more tired with more sleep; give your body a chance to adjust and see what happens.

This is one of those changes you can make right now that makes an immediate difference. You'll notice your energy, focus and straight-up happiness already starting to grow in the first several days.

2. Sing

You've heard that music soothes the savage beast? Well, it can also make you happier! Music triggers the same pleasure centers in your brain that food and sex do and it also looks like the music can be like a mood chiropractor, aligning and realigning you to where you should be. Of course, the same power can be used against you! You are what you eat? How about you are what you listen to?

One neuroscientist, Istvan Molnar-Szakacs, from UCLA, says that the "in terms of brain imaging, studies have shown listening to music lights up, or activates, more of the brain than any other stimulus we know." If you're into lifting weights, music is like the squat of powerlifting —the more you do it the stronger your whole body gets!

I'm not a scientist but I know that there are certain songs that I can listen to when I'm down that have the power to lift me up and make me happy. One 2006 study that supports this found that listening to your favorite songs boosts dopamine activity, that brain chemical related to desire and reward.

There are even studies that suggest that music will lower your heart rate and blood pressure and some music is even being used in the treatment of cancer and strokes.

There are so many studies and research suggesting that planning and designing a special "Happy Playlist" and listening to it daily is so good for you that it would be foolish to not give this a shot. In fact, close this book for thirty minutes and listen to your favorites right now and enjoy!

3. Smile

Here is one external action that directly stimulates a positive internal reaction. Try it and see what happens. Go ahead, smile. No, really. Not for that milli-second moment. Give it a good ten seconds of smiling and see what happens. Laugh with it a little. If someone is next to you, smile at them and see what happens. Was there a little bump in overall well-being? It just did for me as I'm writing this. Now, imagine doing that throughout the day. Can you see the benefit?

Smiling is a vitamin.

There are people, and I'm one of them, that try to eat at regular intervals and take certain nutraceuticals with my meals to maintain peak physical energy levels. What I'm saying here is that if we include regular dosages of "Vitamin Smile" life is going to get much better.

Go out today and smile at fifty people and see what happens to them and, more importantly, to you.

4. Serve

I'm not talking tennis practice here. (Though that can help, too. More on that later.) Serving others, giving to others, helps you get happier. I know it sounds self-serving and a little manipulative but it's a win-win all around. The people you serve are happy and you're happy. What in the world is wrong with that?

Service doesn't have to mean you join the Peace Corps. It's more of a mindset that transfers into physical behaviors. Try something simple like opening the door for someone at a restaurant or holding the elevator. If you want to get more ambitious or need stronger levels volunteer to help anywhere—at church, a homeless shelter or a hospital, coach sports for kids or sign-up with the Red Cross.

If you are an artist or designer, find an organization that can use your skills. Carpenter? Plumber? Same thing. Learn to serve with what you have and do and it will become a natural part of you.

Look around with service eyes. The possibilities are everywhere.

5. Set Goals

One thing that almost all the studies I've researched about increasing happiness agree on is the power of setting goals to change your attitude.

I strongly recommend you start with small, achievable targets that are short duration, quick victories. If you're trying to fill your happiness tank these quick wins provide direct, intravenous shots of happy. What you want to avoid is that downward spiraling path that comes from setting impossible or difficult goals that you can't hope to achieve.

Rather than set a goal of "Save $100,000 this year for retirement" take the gist of it and reframe it to "Save $12.45 by making my coffee at home this week rather than buying it at the cafe."

6. Change Your Routine

If you're a very routinized person and your routine is contributing to low happiness levels (that is, you're unhappy and have been for a while) change something. It'll create discomfort and discomfort is good; especially, if your current comfort level is producing lots of unhappiness. Staying in your old routine is "wallowing" and, yes, it's not comfortable or easy but you won't get clean staying in the mud.

Try some of these:
- Change the way you drive to and from work.
- Change the order of your morning ritual.
- Do you work out in the afternoon? Work out in the morning.
- Do you drink coffee? Drink tea. (Or nothing or vice versa.)
- Eat breakfast. (Or, skip breakfast.)
- Don't eat all day. (Really. It won't kill you to not eat for a day and it might jump start something in your head. For sure you'll appreciate breakfast tomorrow!)
- Turn off your computer.
- Stop interacting with whatever social network you're addicted to, go outside and look at the stars or the clouds (depending on the time of day).

You get the idea. If you're always doing something and it's a regular part of what you do, and you're not getting the results you expected (or need) change it.

Does it make you feel uncomfortable? Good. You're on the right track.

7. Eat Happy Foods (and I Don't Mean Those Funny Brownies)

Nutritionists tell us there are foods that are mood altering AND legal. We'll get more into food in the Health section later but I want you to recognize that food affects your mood and I'm not talking about the absence or presence of it—although, my being hungry has contributed to my being unhappy in the past.

One report I just read suggested that eating fish of any kind, canned, fresh, cooked or raw, was number one on the list of foods that can make you happy. The main ingredient there was those important omega-3s so if you don't like fish there's always capsules.

Chocolate. Just writing the word makes me happy. Don't get crazy on the bars, and the darker the better, but do indulge here. I'm not a big wine drinker but visualizing a night in a log cabin with a fireplace, a glass of red wine, some soft music, some dark chocolate and my favorite people—ahh, happiness.

8. Spend Time With People Who Matter

Building off that last point, one of the biggest happiness elevators, both up and down, are people. Be with people who are going to make you happy. Proactively schedule time with them. It doesn't have to be "quality time"; it just has to be time.

These are the people who give your life meaning. When there's more meaning in your life there's correspondingly more happiness. Period.

Neglect this and you are on the list of people to be pitied.

9. Clean Something, Anything

Sometimes it's hard to be happy when your desk, car or house is so messy and unorganized it looks like you could be a reality television show. This one may be a shocker to my wife but here goes: Clean something.

Pick a drawer. Open it up and toss things out. Take three minutes now and try it. Don't get all crazy and clean everything, just do a drawer or one section of your desk.

Feel better? You should. Organizing the world around us gives us a sense of accomplishment and increases our sense of control. This quick success increases our confidence which can lead to greater security which in turn contributes to our happiness.

Go ahead and clean something else now if you need to. I understand. Hey—maybe my desk is a "little" messy because I'm so happy all the time?

10. LOL!

Feeling down? Sometimes when I'm unhappy I actually feel as though I want to stay there. Sort of like probing at that sore tooth; it's kind of weird, I know, but sometimes I want to stay down. I perpetuate that "down-ness" by reading a sad book or watching a movie I KNOW is a tragedy.

There is a place for cathartic release and I'm not against it but if you've been down for a while you need to get up and those kind of stories aren't going to help.

Instead pick a comedy, look for your favorite brainless, slapstick actor, kick back and let yourself literally laugh-out-loud! Or go to a live comedy show with your friends (see #8 above).

Watch or read something that makes you laugh. Laughing is so very good for you. Don't deny yourself.

11. Stop Doing the Things You Don't Like

This will be short and sweet. If you're doing things that make you unhappy, stop. This includes your job. Household chores qualify, too. Find someone else to do it. Pay someone to do it. Do whatever it takes to not do what makes you unhappy.

Think about this. How does it even make sense? Why would we continue to do things that we KNOW make us unhappy? It's self-sabotaging.

Usually I've kept doing things in the past that made me unhappy because I felt obligated or guilty if I didn't do it. Obligation and guilt are not the values I want to be operating my life from. I persisted in the destruction of my own happiness. Foolish me.

Now, let's be sensible. If you're doing something that makes you unhappy but you and only you can do this and it is something that MUST BE DONE, don't stop abruptly and go eat chocolate. Figure out a plan to work your way out in a fashion that doesn't wreck your life. This is good advice if you're in a job you hate and have bills to pay.

You don't have to be a martyr to be happy.

12. Do the D

Happiness running low? Go outside. Be in the sun (if you have some). You don't have to go for a walk but it wouldn't hurt. There's something that happens when we're outside that can't happen under a roof. Maybe it's the expansiveness, the sweeping vistas (even in the city) or the wind in our face. It's uplifting.

If you can, and you have access, a half-day hike in the mountains is refreshing. Even a suburban downtown hike can help.

One mood altering supplement to consider is vitamin D. It's almost/sort of what you would've received if you took a long walk on the beach on beautiful, sunny day in Hawai'i—just in tablet form and without all the beautiful scenery.

13. Move

With this one I'm not suggesting you move houses or apartments, though that might be required for some extreme circumstances. The moving we're looking at here is physical activity. Go do something, get up and move somewhere. Take a walk, jog, surf, play tennis, basketball or golf. Go do something.

When you're in the midst of the physical activity it's almost like a period of active meditation. It's hard to be negative and brood when you're sweating and gasping for air.

14. Stop

This is the complete opposite of #13 above. Where the previous recommendation was move and be active, this one is stop and be still.

There have been a lot of studies tracking brain activity during prayer and meditation and they're all positive. It's not easy to do, this quieting of the brain, this focus and attention. I would treat it like a workout and go slow in the beginning starting out with a three-minute period. Sound easy? Might be for you. No problem. Go a little longer, then a little longer. After your first week do a "max effort" and see how long you can meditate for.

Prayer and meditation are similar but there are some distinctions that we'll talk about later in the spiritual strength section to follow. One way to look at it (and there are many) is that meditation seeks to empty one's mind whereas prayer is a more pointed and directed focus.

Prayer times are introspective times and useful for identifying course corrections, interpersonal and relational issues, providing times for thanksgiving and gratitude as well as simply being in the presence of the divine.

Again, there are lots of different ways to do both prayer and meditation. Don't get hung up on the religiosity of the recommendation and don't knock it 'til you've tried it.

Some Specific Don'ts

Wanting to keep this section more on the positive I hesitated to include "don'ts" in this list but...there are a couple of super important things that I think you should NOT do so much, if at all, in order to protect your happiness levels.

* Don't Watch Television (So Much)

Turn it off! Unplug. Call the cable company and tell them you don't want service anymore. Television is most analogous to junk food for the brain—at least the way most people use it. I agree and understand that there are deep, meaningful, insightful, educational and—keeping with the recommendation to watch things that make you laugh—funny shows on television. It's just like there are healthy foods in the supermarket and, like that supermarket, guess which aisle people push their carts through? Yep, the sugary, highly processed, unhealthy stuff.

There's so much "mindless, turn on the TV, sit down, grab a beer and watch a sitcom" lifestyle around us that it's no wonder our situation is so dire.

If you're going to watch television at least plan it out. Get your calendar and put in the days and times of your favorite shows or upcoming events and turn the set on only when it's on your calendar. Again, comparing this to eating, there are a lot of people around who advocate for planned meals throughout the day for your physical health. Do the same for your happiness.

If you really want to get into this call the cable company and cancel your account with them. (They'll probably offer you a discounted rate so if anything this can save you some money if you decide to keep it.) There are some services now like Netflix (which I use) or Redbox (which I don't but think looks cool) that have great offerings for both movies and television shows. There are great online providers that offer movies on demand and even my Xbox allows me to watch movies now.

There's so much that's similar between television and eating. When I plan and prepare my food in advance I eat better. The key is planning. Take time to think about what you want to consume in food and, in this case, media.

Maybe you can try it out for a month or so and see what happens. Check it, assess the impact on your life and make whatever changes are in alignment with where you want to be.

Don't Read the News (So Much)

I'm recommending limited news consumption (newspapers, magazines, rss feeds or television) overall because of the excess of negativity in the coverage. I rarely hear of births but always (as in every time I watch or read the newspaper) hear of deaths. There's always some bad thing that happened, something terrible, and it always makes the news. Some new scandal, catastrophe, crisis, or disaster is happening right now as you read this and when you read the paper or turn on the TV you'll hear about it right up front. Day after day, week after week, month after month and year after year of this constant barrage of "down" and it's no wonder I can't get up.

But what if I miss something important? Tim Ferris, in his book, The Four-Hour Work Week, had a great solution: everyone else around you. He says that if it's important enough you'll hear about it from your friends, co-workers or other news/negativity consumers. Trust me, you'll hear about who is dating or broke up with whom as well as the truly vital and sometimes, emergency, information.

Recently, we had a tsunami warning here in Hawai'i. Not having television, I figured out what was happening from noticing our neighbors packing up to evacuate! I turned on a weather app on my phone and got the scoops, then got more information online. About an hour later, the warning system blasted its screeching siren statewide! We were ready and prepared and more than survived without the traditional news channels.

No worries about missing out on the up-to-date information here.

Don't Surround Yourself with Unhappy, Toxic People (So Much)

Toxic people are all around us. Some we can't avoid because we work with them or *sigh* live with them. As an aside, the best way to change someone else is— wait, there is no best way. Don't even try. Instead, focus on yourself. You're a person who also may find it hard to change directions, but at least you can get your hands on the steering wheel.

Where you can, limit your toxic people intake. If you are regularly active in the recommendations in this chapter you'll be getting some balancing positivity in your life but you still want to monitor your contacts.

Think I'm being too harsh? Don't want to stop hanging out with your ol' school buddies? Hey, if you are happy with what your life has been producing thus far, keep on doing the same ol' things with the same ol' people. It's up to you. It always has been.

These recommendations all come down to choices we make and are responsible for.

The people we hang out with the most will have the most influence over us. Look around at your normal circle of contacts. Are they where you want to be and doing what you want to be doing? Do you look at them and see the same level of commitment to living *pono*? If not, you'll find the journey a difficult one.

I won't say it's impossible to get where you want to go but…

Don't Hold Grudges (at All!)

I could have phrased this more in the positive, as in, "Do forgive," but think there's more emphasis here in with the other negatives. There's a great proverb that says a lack of forgiveness is like drinking poison and waiting for the other person to die. I've also read that it is like holding your breath and hoping the other person suffocates.

Both of these sayings communicate the same thing: forgive or die.

You may not drop dead right now but studies have shown that long-term bitterness and unforgiveness affect your health and your happiness—your whole life. Without forgiveness it's impossible to be *pono*.

This requires some internal checking on your part. Or as Ice Cube, back in his ol' school rap days, would say, "You better check yourself before you wreck yourself."

Look inside and identify those people who have wronged you or hurt you and whom you may be holding something against. It's a red flag if you see the person and your pulse starts to race, your smile turns down and your previous sunny disposition is radically changed to cloudy with an increasing chance of thunder and lightning. Sometimes just someone else's mentioning a name will trigger a response in you that may identify unresolved issues.

The process of forgiveness can be as simple as saying that you choose to release your anger, pain and bitterness. Yes, this is one of those "easier to say than do" kind of things, but is it is definitely worth it. Get help from a counselor or friend if you can't do it alone.

I don't want to skim over this but do want to warn you of the dangers inherent here. I've been on both ends of this kind of situation—the side where I've been hurt and the other end where I've hurt others. I've not forgiven and been not forgiven and have experienced the consequences.

Forgiveness is not easy but it is vital. Each of us will have to figure out how to navigate this emotional mine field to get to the side of *pono*.

Again, try some of these recommendations for a couple of weeks or a month. Keep a journal or notebook with your mood and happiness evaluations so you can collect some data. With your record-keeping in place you'll be able to better understand what adds and subtracts to your attitude and overall level of life enjoyment.

Balance is key here. You don't have to cold-turkey stop watching the nightly news but do make sure to balance out that guaranteed dose-of-downer-feeds with some positive intakes. Garbage in, garbage out. Negative in, negative out. Change your inputs and you'll change your life.

This, of course, is not limited to happiness inputs. The importance of what we take in is equally important when we look at the elements of strength.

12
PONO STRONG

Are you strong?

Like "Are you happy?" here's another yes or no question that is fundamental to a *Sense of Power*. But here again, we're faced with an ambiguous, multifaceted word. Let me clarify my definition.

> ***Strength is the sum capacity of physical, mental, relational and spiritual health and power.***

I feel strong when I'm able to say that I can bring any and all of these four elements to bear when needed or desired.

Are you strong?

If you're like me, the yes/no answer scale leaves you begging for a "sometimes/mostly/maybe" checkbox. Also, if you're like me, this health gauge is an ebb and flow, it's one that can be filled or emptied and, therefore, nurtured or neglected.

And if we're like each other we've had times when our gauge was noticeably full or noticeably empty.

The big question is can we live in such a way that we are running with a gauge that is always close to a full tank? Short answer—maybe. You can keep your car's gas tank always full—but only if you never drive it. Just turning it on consumes fuel.

The solution then is to track our health and strength gauge and refuel as needed. We want to make sure there's fuel in the tank when we need it. And that only comes from filling up when we don't.

Kalalau: Crawl In, Swim Out?
Who would've thought one backpacking trip could pack in so many tests and lessons?

A couple of years back my family and a few friends went on a hiking and camping trip to the beautiful garden isle of Kauaʻi. We called ourselves the Kalalau 9 after the name of our target beach and the number of our crew—me, my wife, two sons and five really good friends. In front of us lay an all-day eleven-mile hike into an incredibly remote and breathtaking beach called Kalalau on Kauaʻi's Na Pali coast. We planned to spend three days sleeping under the stars and enjoying the beauty before another full day's hike back out to civilization. Going to Kalalau has always been on my to-do dream list and it was finally going to happen.

Looking forward to a grueling experience I felt healthy and confident in every way that I could make it.

Physically, I had been working out consistently and intensely in ways that regularly tested and taxed me to my limits. Those limits were not just identified in the physical but in the mental as well. The workouts were varied and unpredictable and often were more mentally challenging than physically. They would mess with my mind and I'd find myself in the middle of the workout, wanting to cry, quit and curl up in the corner. To this day I'm not sure what has been strengthened more, my body or my mind through these intense demands.

Relationally, I was making this hike with people that I had known for years. I've trusted and been through things with them that had strengthened bonds and assured me I could count on them for support and encouragement. In fact, we had all partnered to help each other spiritually as well.

The hike in took us much longer than we expected. Maybe it was my wife's sprained knee at mile ten or having to flag a passing fishing boat and swim out together through thunderous surf to hitch a ride. Maybe. Or maybe it was the eight-mile mark—where the trail narrowed and could be measured in inches with a rock wall on one side and a 500-foot drop off to the ocean below on the other— that slowed us down. Maybe.

That stretch of trail caused me some of the most intense parental stress I've ever had as a father. The trail there had a name and it was called "Crawler's Ledge." My youngest son, twelve years old at the time, and I were at the rear of our group with my wife and oldest son at the front. As I watched them in the lead carefully and painstakingly pick their way along the ledge my heart started beating faster and faster, pounding ferociously all the way up in my ears.

We hadn't even edged on to the ledge and already I was starting to stress out.

I could visualize, and I wished I couldn't, all the worst possible catastrophes that could happen. I imagined my son slipping in front of me and starting to slide down towards the crashing waves, beyond my outstretched hands, with nothing and nobody to help! There's no way I could watch so I imagined myself having to dive after him with the hope of getting hung up on a ledge before we hit bottom!! My wife would be a widow and my other son and daughter fatherless!!! It would be, it could be, it shouldn't be...!!!!

Whoa, easy there. Whew...

I seriously had those thoughts and seriously had to get them under control before taking that first step onto the ledge. You may think I was overreacting, or maybe it wasn't that bad when you went, but having my family on the trail changed the whole situation for me. I felt like a negligent father for exposing my kids to that ledge.

Now, I know there were people who safely traversed this part of the trail, no problem. In fact, we had met two women coming up the trail from Kalalau so I knew it was possible. But we had also re-met two guys who had passed us earlier in the day who turned around and were heading back after seeing that ledge. Hmmm...

Before we took our first step I reviewed where we were (there on the edge!), where we had come from and where we were heading. I knew my son was ready because we had all put in the physical miles over the previous months. We'd also experienced challenging things as a family that had strengthened us mentally and relationally as a family. I was hesitantly confident (can I say that?), cautiously optimistic, when we started because I believed that we had filled up our tanks. Who would've thought that the hike itself would be a tank-filler??

Most of the rest of that crawl is foggy and only dimly recalled. I remember trying to appear calm with my insides churning and my brain still conjuring up all the calamitous possibilities. We all made it safely to the other end of the ledge where it widened out to a normal (and way safer) trail. After taking a rest break to drink water and stop all our legs from quivering, we were quiet, knowing that we had just shared something that tested, defined and marked us for life.

Re-CREATE-ion

The way our bodies seem to work is with movement—movement back and forth between fullness and emptiness. We move, we do, we expend energy (whether mental, physical, relational or spiritual), and as we move we empty—sometimes slowly, sometimes quickly.

We stop moving, we stop doing, we rest, we reset, we gather energy—sometimes slowly, sometimes quickly.

This is that aforementioned ebb and flow of life. It's the natural, and sustainable, cycle of *pono*. When we are living this way we live in a system of continuous creation and re-creation, a cycling of inputs and outputs, allowing us to fulfill the mandate that is our *Sense of Purpose*.

This idea of replenishing and recreating is how I understand the Jewish idea of the Sabbath. It was originally designed to provide rest for people, land and livestock so there could be abundance at all times and through all seasons. Most people think of it as a single day, the seventh day, whether Saturday or Sunday, when in some cases it was the seventh or even the fiftieth year! Whatever and however it's defined, it was and still is, a time of rest.

The Sabbath concept takes a long-term view of life and we would be foolish to ignore it.

Farmers understand this better than most. You can't keep planting and harvesting, planting and harvesting, season after season, on the same patch of ground. There must be a time when that field is left fallow, plowed but deliberately unsown, to allow the land to refresh and regain its ability to produce. If you skip the replenishing process there may be a harvest this season and maybe even the next, but don't expect seasons of plenty to follow.

Our own ability to produce is at risk whenever our health is not given this opportunity; we are not *pono* and it shows. But when we have these elements of strength in our life, when we have our physical, mental, relational, and spiritual pieces in alignment, we have what's needed for a strong *Sense of Power*.

We expend energy on our journey and recognize that we have to use gas if we want to drive. We need to also recognize that without stopping to fill our tank, the journey will come to a sputtering, dragging, unceremonious end. If we press on the pedal and there's no gas we're not moving anywhere no matter how clear the goal, how strongly we believe, how badly we want it. No amount of happy thoughts makes up for a lack of fuel.

It sounds like a no-brainer but there needs to be something in the tank and refueling doesn't just happen. Re-creation needs to happen deliberately. We need to protect our our health.

> **Re-creation needs to happen deliberately. We need to protect our our health.**

The ancient Hawaiians incorporated a codified system of laws called the *kapu* system. This system regulated just about every aspect of life for every level of society. Most understand the word to mean taboo or prohibited—what one could or could not do or eat or not eat for example. In fact, contemporary usage generally connotes a strict "No Trespassing!" sort of feeling.

However, the word also includes deeper meanings of something sacred or consecrated and even sanctified. The concept here is of a place or an object that was set apart, protected, for a special and specific reason or activity.

Often specific *kapu* were enacted to protect certain species of fish or animals in order to ensure sustainability and their survival. The Hawaiians lived in a society where these rules were taken seriously. Persons who were were caught fishing during a *kapu* season were sometimes punished with death.

Now, relating this to our own health, I'm not saying death sentences should be meted out for rule violations or infractions! What I am suggesting is that our heath, our strength, our ability to produce needs to be protected in the same way and with the same sense of urgency.

The following sections will address my approach and thoughts for developing strength in the areas of the physical, mental, relational and spiritual aspects of our lives. When these pieces are in place there is strength. When there is strength there is *pono*.

Our responsibility to create and re-create deliberately, to set up a sort of *kapu* system that recognizes activities and behaviors, needs to be in place for our lives to be sustainable and abundant.

I read tons of articles and books on this sort of thing and guess I should say talk to a physician before you do any crazy health changes. I would also recommend finding a friend you trust who IS healthy and ask them what they're doing. Begin to believe what you see and feel.

Check your current condition. Do the lab work, check your blood pressure, weight and body fat. Give yourself a solid "before" picture, a baseline, from these tests. In fact, take a couple of pictures of yourself in your swimsuit for comparison later.

Understand that I artificially slice up the concept of health and strength into four pieces I'm labeling physical, mental, relational and spiritual for better organization. In the real world all four are rooted and linked together. If one aspect is weak, the others are affected. Inversely, when one is strengthened all are strengthened.

All four of these elements work together to produce the concept of strength and health as I understand it. It's one egg that is made up of the shell, yolk and albumen (egg whites); they are synergistic. As with the section on happiness, I'll begin with some broad principles then narrow down to specific health practicalities.

KA'ALA SOUZA

13
ZOMBIE PREPPERS

If you want to be able to move when you need to, you must move when you don't want to. Sometimes that couch and television are *waaayyy* more compelling than that sweaty workout. Still, to put it a little crassly in self-defense terms, it's better to sweat on the mat than bleed on the street. You have to put in the time to get strong in every area.

Ever since we saw the movies Shaun of the Dead and Zombieland my kids and I have joked around about different zombie invasion scenarios. We'd ask questions like "What's the top speed of zombies and would we be able to outrun them?" When I'd work out with my boys I'd point out the practical zombie survival aspects of the exercises we were doing to motivate them and get a laugh. (Really, more for the laugh.)

We were joking—but only sort of. The joking was centered around a zombie-end-of-the-world scenario. The reality is the need to be prepared for day-to-day as well as emergency and unpredictable demands. You can't expect your body and mind to hold up under intense demands if you haven't given it less intense doses to practice and develop from. I want to know that when I need to reach deep into my supply tank of strength, whether physical, mental, relational or spiritual, that there will be enough to get me through.

The principles of health are very similar to the principles outlined for happiness, at least the first two are, because, as with all things *pono*, they're woven and linked together.

1. Want It

It's hard to get strong if you don't want to. It sounds like another no-brainer but you'd be surprised at how many people show up at the gym who really don't want to be there. You don't have to be 110% motivated every day but, in those quiet, introspective moments when you're looking at your future and your life, you have to identify health as a priority and make it happen.

Realize that for your life vision to become a reality you must be able to generate and sustain enough energy and power to get you there and your health is your fuel.

2. Live It

Living *pono* leads to better health. You cannot be *pono* without being healthy, and when you're healthy you have a shot at being *pono*. The food you eat, your exercise routines, your attitude towards the people and environment around you all need to be right and in their proper place, in alignment and in balance.

3. Take Care of Yourself First

There is no future if you don't take care of your present. This sounds selfish and many, many, many people I talk to feel guilty when they devote time and effort to taking care of themselves. They're well-meaning but myopic, good hearted but short-sighted.

Taking care of your health is not selfish. The real selfishness is denying the people around you your full and complete presence. You may be there for the short-term but won't be around to see your grandchildren because you didn't take care of yourself today. That's selfish.

Even the airlines recognize this principle when they instruct us, in an emergency, to put our own breathing masks on first then help those with us. It's not selfish, it's wisdom. Real selfishness is when the failure to take care of yourself leads to unmet and unfulfilled expectations, dreams and hopes for the future.

4. Have a Clear Vision For Your Health

This is definitely one of the big key principles. You need to visualize what the future would look like if you were fully engaged physically, mentally, relationally and spiritually in the world around you. This is a workout in itself but a workout that needs to be done to help sustain your efforts.

5. Change it Up

Everything works but not everything works forever. I heard that quote somewhere and it was in relation to physically working out and exercising. The idea is that just because you lost 30 pounds walking around your block or playing basketball three times a week or standup paddling (here in Hawai'i that's a big thing) don't think that you will continue to be challenged enough to get the same results.

If you weren't doing anything before you started whatever you started, than anything you do will create enough of a stimulus in your body to produce the weight loss.

I've found this applies to every aspect of health including, and maybe especially, spiritual health.

I'm definitely not against routines and good habits but if growth and development are the goal and I'm not growing or developing, then I can't keep the sacred cow around just because I've "always done it this way." Change is good.

6. Workout Your Will (Power)

Where there's a will, you will find a way. Work on strengthening your willpower before you're hit by temptation. In other words, if during your morning planning session you've decided to work out late that afternoon, call some of your friends and have them meet you at the park or the gym or wherever you work out. That'll make it that much harder to back out on the plan. I've found it's much, much easier to break an appointment with myself than with someone else. Of course you can still call and cancel but it's harder to do.

I think of this as tricking myself to show up and even though I know that I know that I know I'm doing this—it still works.

Here's another example: Say you have a bunch of cookies someone gave you as a gift sitting on the table in your house and you're trying to cut sugar and calories. In the morning after a good hearty breakfast the temptation to eat those cookies may be lower. (May be. I love cookies all the time so this is always difficult!) Don't wait to try your willpower when you come home from work, tired, exhausted and starving! Dump them down the drain now! Or, take them to work and give them to your co-workers who don't care about sugar. They'll thank you for your consideration and your health will thank you for your determination. You may regret it later when you come home and kick yourself for tossing them BUT you won't eat any cookies because they're not there!

What more and more research is telling us is that we can strengthen our will-power just like a muscle. So work it out.

7. Be Flexible and Creative

Make plans but be willing to change them. Don't get hung up on not having the right equipment or gear or software or time. Look around—the possibilities are there all around you to move and be healthy.

8. Don't Get Religious (in a Bad Way)

What I mean by this is don't get all down and guilty on yourself and beat yourself up over a missed workout or get-together with friends. You're in this for the long-term so a missed workout day or week or month is a drop in the proverbial life bucket. There are even times when you want to deliberately miss workouts for a couple of weeks or do half the plan to let your body, mind or spirit recover.

Also, don't get down on other people and judge them because they're not eating like you or working out like you, going to church like you or doing something else that you're doing that you think they should do. That's the worse kind of religion and I've seen this at the gym, at restaurants and at church; it's no fun for anyone.

Listen to your body—it'll tell you when you need a break or when you need to ramp up the intensity. Listen to your soul; it will tell you the same thing. As you practice these *pono* principles of health, you'll find the strength you need accessible and available in the day-to-day moments as well as in those times of crisis. There will be gas in the tank when you step on that pedal.

14
PONO AS RX'D

The following four sections are what I call the *pono* prescription for developing our *Sense of Power*. Each of the four, the physical, mental, relational and spiritual, start out by providing a definition of what each part means followed by a set of practical things to do (and not do). It's not truly prescriptive in a dogmatic or absolute sense, but more of an expanding or experimenting approach to this sort of thing.

The definition allows for evaluation and focus. The prescriptions of dos and don'ts are best practices that I have found most helpful and productive. When I'm living *pono* like this, strengthening and refueling my whole self, I'm energized and active around my purpose and priorities.

Physical Strength: If You Can Run, You Won't Have to Hide

It's hard to hide the absence of physical health.

The absence of balance is in your face and in your gut. I can fake my lack of happiness and put on a smile to pretend it's all good but no amount of vertical stripes is going to make me look good when I'm not. No makeup will change the numbers at the doctor's office or on the scale. There's nowhere to run and nowhere to hide when I'm not *pono* physically.

Like any other state of balance sometimes the smallest breath of wind or that last straw or single grain of sand can disturb the setup. Eating food without the nutrients necessary for your body to function is disruptive to your body's equilibrium. Likewise, poor sleep patterns, exercise, or excessive stress can bring our carefully balanced bodies to our knees, literally and figuratively. One of the reasons many take this less seriously than they should is that the bad outcomes are not always immediately evident. The negative consequences of a poor diet may not manifest until years later when it may be too late to do anything about it.

Attempting to define physical strength and health is a challenging activity. It's not about how fast or long you can run, though it is. It's also not about how much weight you can lift over your head, though it is. It's all the above and then some.

A friend of mine described it as having no limitations to living an active, fulfilled life. Another told me health is having our bodies respond positively to our treatment and nurture of it. One simply said health is having the energy required for living.

I'm thinking that we all need to have some sort of measuring stick, a sort of definitional baseline for physical health that allows us to track where we are and how we're doing with this category. For me, being physically healthy means that I can say:

I am capable of doing and moving where, when and how I want and need to.

Another way to think about this is that my physical health doesn't limit my dreams and desires. I want to know that I have enough in my tank to get me where I'm supposed to go and allow me to do the tasks I need to do.

For myself, I had to have in my definition the understanding that physical health is having the capacity to move when I need to, not just when I want to. I recognize that my motivation fluctuates and if I'm only going to work towards increasing my capacity when I want to, there's going to be a lot more couch days than gym days!

Physical strength and health are about action and movement. The actions and movements on the inside support the actions and movements on the outside.

Here are the basic, practicals you should have in place to move towards *pono* in your physical health.

1. Move More

Whatever movement you want or can currently do go ahead and do. Then do it some more. We are a country that doesn't ask for much from our bodies. Through the day our bodies may be required to move from bed to bathroom to kitchen to car to office to desk and back. Your mileage may differ but for a lot of years that was mine.

All the tips you've heard about getting out more, playing with your kids, walking with friends or taking the stairs are all good stuff. Pick something and do it, then do it some more.

Don't think you need to go run a marathon to get started; there's no need to get crazy! There are lots of low-barrier-to-entry things you can do to get moving. I like those dance games on the video game consoles. I can get my heart rate up pretty quickly dancing along with the game. The Wii video game console has boxing games and fitness games that will give your body some healthy stress if you're not currently active. And it's fun. It won't get you ready for that marathon or a Ultimate Fighting Championship match but at least you're doing something.

The key thing is to keep moving. If the video games get boring change it up and do some real kick-boxing or dancing at the club. I cycle through three or four different workout programs a year, kind of along the lines of the old "muscle confusion principle."

Start keeping a movement section in your journal or on your computer's calendar. You'll be encouraged as you look back and see where you were.

Whatever you find to do, do it. Then, do it some more.

2. Sleep More

There are truckloads of research and debate on just how much is enough sleep. Before you say, well, I can get by with only three hours of sleep a night, understand that your objective shouldn't be to "get by" but to thrive and flourish. There are some plants in my garden that survive and get by for days when I forget to water them but that's not what they need to achieve full growth.

As I said in the earlier section, each person is going to function better at different sleep levels. Some will perform excellently at six hours while others are in zombie mode with anything less than eight. Keep a record of how many hours you get each night (or day if you work the graveyard shift which is a completely different story) for a couple of weeks, noting your mood and energy levels next to the hours of sleep. Find what works for you and make it habit.

3. Eat (More) Healthy Food

Hippocrates, the father of medicine, said "Let your food be your medicine and your medicine be your food."

Garbage in, garbage out. Do expect higher energy levels, increased productivity and better overall performance from your body's engine when you put in higher octane fuel. Don't be surprised when you're constantly feeling sluggish, down, depressed and slow when you're putting in garbage.

What's garbage?

Now, here again there is so much conflicting information out there revolving around what is healthy and what isn't. There's always a new diet from this beach's, country's or doctor's new book all with research, recipes and DVDs to get you started.

If you're like me, you probably don't have the science chops to debate with these diet marketers so who to believe? I don't know for certain but I am thinking that if my food choices contain ingredients that I can't spell, explain or produce myself (if I had to) the simple conclusion is I'm not going to ingest it.

As much as possible I've been living off of a couple of practical, self-explanatory, and kind of hipster principles:

- Eat food that spoils
- Eat food from local providers
- Eat at regular intervals
- Drink lots of water
- Supplement wisely

Read, research and experiment. This last thing, the experimenting, requires you to be aware and record what's going on. It's not easy to achieve strong physical health without increased awareness and tracking. Grab a notebook or use your computer to track things like energy and stress levels, workouts and food you eat on a given day. If that sounds like too much work for you now though, ignore it, put it on the back burner and come back to it later. You don't have to track something to do it—it just helps in the future to know how you got to where you got.

Along the lines of getting a little closer to my food I've planted a garden and set up an aquaponics system in my backyard raising tilapia and fertilizing a grow-bed full of herbs, kale, tomatoes and other vegetables. If you are absolutely clueless about gardening like me, but want to give it a shot, check out the "Square-Foot Gardening" method. Easy, fairly inexpensive and it will get you up and growing in no time.

I like what one person told me when they said "Don't be on a diet, change your diet." Change what you eat for a month and see what happens.

Mental Strength: More of Less

Mental strength is a lot like the physical in that it's pretty easy to see when it's not there. It's hard to hide low productivity and that's one of the clearest indicators of a weak mind. By productive I mean your ability to produce what you have purposed to produce whether it's at work or at home, with your checkbook or your waistline. Mental strength, or the absence of it, shows.

Mental health means:

> ***I can address and focus my thoughts where, when and how I want and need to.***

The bible is full of verses encouraging us to have a strong mind.

> " A sound mind makes for a robust body, but runaway emotions corrode the bones."

> "…be transformed by the renewing of your mind…"

> "A person without self-control is like a house with its doors and windows knocked out."

One's ability to bring focus and attention to bear on a problem, situation, or circumstance is directly correlated to one's mental health. Obviously, the stronger you are mentally the healthier you are overall.

The bottom line is: Your mind and how you think affect your body and health.

With so much of our culture focused on attaining more and more, I want to focus this section relating to mental strength on two things you should have less of.

Worry Less

"Don't worry about a thing. 'Cause every little thing is going to be al' right."—Bob Marley

Anxiety and worry are not good for you. Stop worrying. When I was a child I was warned about the dangers of crossing the street, taking candy from strangers, and riptides in the ocean (I grew up in Hawai'i). No one ever warned me about the dangers of high levels of stress, worry and anxiety.

Stress kills. If not as immediate as some other more in-your-face dangers it's just as permanent. There are studies and research out there in the studies and research world that highlight over and over again the potent and deadly effect of stress on our quality and quantity (length of) life.

Most of us are aware that drinking and driving don't mix and if you're going to drink you need to give your car keys to someone else. Why? Because it's dangerous. Duh. Multitasking? Uh, uh. Nope. We've never been told that we need to put down the Blackberries and iPhones, unplug the laptops and release our to-do lists or face the potential negative consequences. No one has ever told us how bad stress, anxiety and worry are for us.

Consider yourself told.

Focusing on my worries takes my focus off where it should be. When my brain is occupied with anxiety and worry it can't simultaneously focus on things like my mission or purpose or even gratitude and appreciation. We almost literally have to beat worry back in our minds and "take captive every thought" that leads us down those defeated, negative paths.

Value stress reduction by putting your money where your stress is. This means spend your time and your money on things that contribute to anti-stress. Commit to that gym membership or buy that P90x DVD. Go ahead and get that new book, pick a rainy day and curl up on the couch. Evaluate the anxiety reducing impact of your purchases (including food) and eliminate items that don't increase your ability to minimize worry and stress.

When you value this your calendar will show it, too. Choose to take that vacation now or that extra comp day off. Schedule in, seriously, write it in your calendar, "walk on the beach with my spouse/kids/friends/by myself" days. Be proactive in valuing those actions and things that bring your stress down.

Value stress reduction by putting your money where your stress is.

Decompress. Leave work early (or at least on time) and instead of heading straight for the freeway, stop by the bookstore, or walk around the block, or head over to the park or gym to let some of the steam out. Be deliberate and aware of what you're doing and understand its importance for mental health.

Scuba divers have a potentially dangerous illness called Decompression Sickness (DCS). It used to be called the "bends" because the pain in your joints and bones would double you over in agony when it hit you. Divers are susceptible to this illness if they are down deep for a long time and, on their way to the surface, don't make the required "decompression stops."

If a diver got the "bends" an extended period in a recompression chamber was called for. The initial treatment provides doses of 100% oxygen to the body. Can you see where I'm headed with this?

Slow down. Make the required stops to smell the roses, coffee or whatever aroma helps you not to worry.

Listen to Bob. Really. Or whatever music relaxes you. Every little thing is going to be all right when you are *pono*.

Do Less

The second thing you need to have less of are tasks. Now, I know this sounds like a pipe-dream but hear me out on this one.

Back in the day "I'm great at multitasking" was the required answer for job hunters wanting to get ahead. Now, the ability to focus, pick out and prioritize the one big thing that needs to be done is key. Single-tasking rules and multitasking drools.

Listen to Bob. Really.

Train yourself to think before you do. Take the list of tasks in front of you and begin to trace back the ones that link to the core objectives of the project, the mission or your life. When you get in the habit of doing this you can whittle the list down to less and less that will accomplish more and more.

The Pareto Rule works here, too. If 20% of the things you're going to do are going to provide 80% of the return on your time investment, then why do the other 80%? Do less to accomplish more.

Learn to say "no" to the things that are not in alignment with who you are or where you're going, the things that are important. Spending time connecting with our *Sense of Place* and *Purpose* clarifies what we need to say "yes" to and what we need to turn away from. When that big picture is clear, our choices and decisions are almost made for us.

Include in your day's start up ritual and routine (along with brushing your teeth and eating, of course) a selection of ONE THING in your day that, if it got done, would move your life forward. Make it a habit to get this "one thing" done daily.

Think about it—365 beneficial "dones" are an awesome accomplishment. Each "one thing" identified by you as important and checked off as done each day will help to motivate and propel you into another and the next. It's one of the secrets of generating an upward spiral of success.

With less on my plate, I get to savor each and every ingredient presented; I can focus because there's less. And when I'm focused, I'm mentally stronger. And when I'm mentally stronger I'm healthier and moving towards getting and staying *pono*.

Relational Strength: Be a Groomer Not a Fighter

Solitary confinement is one of the harshest penalties (outside lethal injection) in all the prison movies I've ever seen. Being alone, in a small cell, with limited movement, interaction or stimulation is what the really, really bad guys get. My thinking is if solitary is that bad, community, being with others, must be that good.

Being relationally strong and healthy is not about having strong interpersonal skills, winning friends and influencing people, but about having strong, real relationships that you can count on.

In today's world of always on, always connected, I'm always surprised when I find people who are weak in this area. We have a thousand friends on our social networks but no one to call when we've lost our job or our marriage is suffering at home. I can read status updates on Twitter any time, day or night, but I can't get deeper than what my "friend" ate or had for breakfast that day. "Always on" leaves me feeling off with quantity over quality, surface over depth.

In over twenty years of pastoring and being involved in people's lives at the intimate moments of birth and death, connection and separation, I've seen this amazing lack of depth over and over and over again.

There was that husband, himself a pastor, who had a secret life he told no one about because there was no one he could trust to accept him as a man rather than a minister. His marriage of many years collapsed in a month under the pressure of that secret. I knew him, I talked to him, I asked him how he was doing every time I saw him. He would have friend requested me on Facebook and maybe even played word games online but he never confided in me, or anyone else, about his struggles. Outwardly he looked and sounded strong but on the inside, where it counted, the absence of, or weaknesses in, the bridges he made with other people couldn't support him.

I remember two teenagers years ago, one who didn't quite fit in and the other the big man on campus. Both tragically took their lives and even now, thinking about them, I'm saddened by that loss and wonder how I could've helped more, or connected better, or did something to provide what was obviously missing.

Am I saying that just having a real friend, someone to confide in and talk to, would've helped prevent these things? Yeah, that's exactly what I'm saying. Having been there, personally, at points in my life where my marriage was stressed or taking my life seemed like the only solution, I'm thankful for those people who were able to enter my solitary confinement cell and lend me their strength.

This is no joke. Your health, your life, depends on the level of interdependence, the relational strength, you have with others.

Relational strength means:

I have positive, mutually strengthening, long-lasting people connections in my life.

Let me break these elements down a little bit more.

Positive

When I use the word positive to describe a relationship it means supportive, encouraging, strengthening, challenging, and uplifting. These are the people in your life that leave you more buoyant, brighter and flat out better when you get together. They will challenge you and say the hard things when necessary to move you forward. These are people you can count on.

Relationships are like food and there's a lot of highly processed, sugary, no nutrient, over manufactured, cheap deals out there for both. You want to select and invest in people who sustain you, are wholesome and natural, and contribute to your energy tank.

On the other hand, you probably have some "friends" who, every time you leave them you feel more down, discouraged and depressed than when you arrived. They're the ones that are always complaining about something or someone, gossiping, finger-pointing (both index and middle) or arguing. Or, they may be the ones that when you hang up the phone after talking with them you're crushed under all the sky-is-falling list of worries and anxieties they've passed on to you.

Now, I'm not saying abandon any of these negative (toxic?) relationships. What I am suggesting is that you recognize your own need for positive inputs from the people you interact with the most. Negative in, negative out; positive in gives positive out and a stronger, healthier you.

Take a sheet of paper and draw a line down the middle with a plus and minus as headings over the two columns. Look through the past couple of months of your calendar and categorize the people you spent time with as "positive-izers" or "negative-izers" and put their names in the appropriate section on the paper. Who do you spend more time with?

Again, food and friends can take the same approach. Choose wisely.

Mutually Strengthening

"Mutually strengthening" means that I'm not talking to my psychologist who is paid to help me but to someone with whom I am also a positive source of support and encouragement—I receive and I give. This is interdependence; I need you and you need me and we have a reciprocal and mutually beneficial commitment to strengthening each other.

This works hand in hand with the description of positive above in that sometimes you will be the one to provide the support, yours will be the shoulder leaned on. It's a quid pro quo—you got my back and I got yours.

Long-Lasting

"Long-lasting" simply means that the relationship is no one night, one month or one year stand but one that has been tested and tried through the spring time and the winter, the fire and the ice. If you've been friends, real friends long enough, you've argued, reconciled, disagreed and compromised through the seasons and that's always good for the relationships. You know you're not getting bullsh*t advice or counsel from someone today who didn't bullsh*t you yesterday.

Time builds trust if you keep it real.

This isn't a section on "How to Win Friends and Influence People" as much as my attempt to emphasize and reinforce the need to have friends and work towards strong relationships in our lives.

Killer Stress
I saw a documentary the other night called Stress: Portrait of a Killer that addressed, of course, the killer nature of stress. The research demonstrated how stress takes years off your life, makes you fatter, and can cause heart disease. It pretty clearly explained how tight the connections are between our physical, mental and emotional states.

One part of this stress documentary focused on research conducted in Africa with baboons.

Turns out the alpha males have much less stress than the submissives in their group. The alphas were the lord of their jungle. They were mean, cruel, and abusive—as far as baboons go. They stood alone, powerful, as the lesser monkeys cringed and huddled together for comfort.

Well, what comes around goes around—you stand alone, you fall alone.

Ten years into the study the group's eating pattern changed after they found a food dump from human workers. One day they consumed contaminated meat and half the baboon tribe was wiped out.

Guess who died?

Yep—all the bossy, loner, aggressive monkeys. The researchers found that the baboons who were in close, frequent contact with other baboons, grooming and touching one another, survived, while those that were alone and solitary died.

I may be reading into the baboon study but it's interesting that the ones who lived were the ones with a stronger sense of community, whose strength was only in, with and through others. The loners, those in their self-inflicted solitary confinement, died how they lived—alone.

This discussion could have been written up in the previous section on mental stress but I think it fits more appropriately here looking at the choices we make to develop lasting and strengthening relationships.

Choose life with, for and because of people and you won't go wrong. Take yourself out of solitary confinement, throw away the key and start grooming.

Spiritual Strength: Sandwiches and Skinny Jeans
I would have liked to say that I'm spiritually healthy when I'm *pono* but I'm not sure how much that would help. After twenty-five years of specifically studying this topic, this is how I define spiritual health and I'm not even sure my definition is at all close to reality. Ask me again after another twenty-five and we'll see.

Here's where I'm at now:

> ***I'm spiritually healthy when there's a sense of positivity in and with the world around me.***

When I was younger I thought I "knew" a lot more about this but the more I see the less I actually "know." What I do know is that when I'm closely connected to the impossible and inexplicable I'm stronger spiritually. The more I try to define and systemize the spiritual the further away I get from it. The more I try to codify, pigeon-hole and wrap my mind around it the less I'm able to actually embrace and feel my spirituality. To define and categorize is to make the eternal temporal and the intangible touchable and I'm not sure if that's a good thing.

With that way-out, touchy-feely, loosey-goosey introduction I still want to—really more like have to—share some practicals for increasing our spiritual strength. To be *pono* is to be spiritual. When I'm connected and correct with both the tangible and intangible world around me I am in a state of rightness and I'm strong. This strength gets me through, to, over, above and beyond whatever I'm facing.

A few years back I read an article about two spiritual leaders whom I knew personally. Both were facing trying and difficult circumstances and both had hit the proverbial wall. In the midst of their struggles they realized that the spiritual system they had in place wasn't providing the power necessary to carry them through the challenges. To me it was kind of like they were solar powered outdoor lights left in the shade—they still had some light shining, but it was low and flickering.

Each took different routes to refill their spiritual energy tanks. The thing that struck me was how deliberate this process was for them. Both knew the importance, identified the shortfall then set out to do something about it. Sitting on the couch doesn't get you in shape physically and, guess what, it doesn't work for your soul either.

After reading the article two big questions came up for me:

- If the spiritual professionals were struggling, what can the rest of us do to maintain and grow our own spiritual health?

- How do I know if I'm spiritually healthy in the first place?

The first question deals with activities and behaviors while the second deals with definition and measurement. There is a TON (literally with the books, magazines, audio tapes/CD, videos and people) of material out there detailing activities for every race and religion but it is difficult to pin down exactly what we are supposed to look like AFTER we've completed the program.

Let me address the second question of how to know what spiritually healthy looks like by looking.

Spiritual Sandwiches?

Subway Sandwiches does a great job of giving us a before/after picture of what you get after their food with the "Jared" commercials. There was one commercial that showed a guy, Jared, who had lost weight by eating Subway's sandwiches, holding up an enormous pair of jeans next to his new Subway-fed jeans and the difference, the change, was drastic. I'm not sure if their weight-loss program was what produced the new Jared but the "after" vision was clear: new, way smaller, jeans!

What's So Funny 'Bout Peace, Love and Understanding??

Midnight Oil is a political rock band out of Australia that I saw in concert here in Honolulu many, many years ago. They played a song that night that became one of my favorites ever called "What's So Funny 'Bout Peace, Love and Understanding?" It was a cover from a guy named Nick Lowe who first wrote it for Elvis Costello.

The title is the hook and the answer to the lyric is "nothing"— there's nothing funny about those three things and when I consider what a clear before/after picture should be of any spiritual health program it must begin with an increase in peace, love and understanding.

Peace

Peace in this case is the cessation of war, both internal and external. When there's no war with myself and those around me I'm healthy. It's when I'm living without threat or fear of attack that I'm living in peace. When I go to work and I don't dread seeing my co-workers and boss or when I walk down my street feeling safe I have this external peace.

Internally, it means that I'm not waging debates with my self about my self. There is *pono* when I'm at peace within.

Love

Love is that feeling of goodwill and the desire to do good for others and the world around us. In Hawaiian, the word aloha connotes this perfectly with its emphasis on compassion, empathy and kindness. Love is a collection and conglomeration of emotions, feelings and characteristics. It's patient, kind, gentle, always hopes and always perseveres. It doesn't bend or alter; neither is it shaken. Love laughs and cries and shares the laughter and the tears.

Understanding

For me understanding stems from recognizing our mutual need for one another. Only in diversity is found interdependence. I'm as incomplete without you as you are without me. Understanding leads to the complementary interaction between us. Where the minutiae separate and divide there is no understanding; where there is no understanding there can be no spiritual strength.

I listed these not in order of importance but rather in the order of the lyrics in the song but there could be one that is of higher priority. In the Christian Bible, faith, hope and love are listed as the things that will remain when all is said and done and when all has come and gone. The greatest of these, though, the priority, is love. Whatever spiritual development approach we adopt, if an increase in love is not in the top three expected outcomes, some serious re-evaluation is called for.

In fact, you can evaluate where you're at with this every day you get in your car, drive, go to work, or to the park. Ask yourself the following questions and check.

• Am I looking out for the good of those around me or only for myself?

• Do I get out of my car after driving in rush hour traffic with my pulse rate still low or did I feel the need to "communicate" strongly with horn and voice to my fellow drivers?

• Does my life include regular contact with people who are different from me or are all like me?

• Does my attitude generally reflect a positive rather than negative aspect?

Making It By Faking It

All right, so there's nothing funny about love and peace and understanding but how exactly do we go about increasing it in our lives? I can track outward "spiritual" actions and/or behaviors but how do I know if what I'm doing is truly reflecting what I'm feeling on the inside? What if I'm just faking it?

Here's a concept for you: praxis. I understand this word loosely to mean practical application, or action, rather than theory or creativity. For us, in this case, we want to be into the doing instead of the contemplating. Let me explain.

I heard a story of a guy who went to visit a counselor because he had fallen out of love with his wife. The therapist asked the man what he would do if he still loved his wife. His "what-I-would-do-if-I-still-loved-her-list" included roses, regular dinner dates, love notes and more time together.

The counselor instructed the guy to spend the next month doing exactly those things.

When the husband returned for his follow-up session he announced that he wouldn't be coming back for further appointments because he was now deeply in love with his wife again and had no need for counseling.

Praxis is the Nike motto of just *doing* it. Something happens, something changes in our spirit, when we act upon something, when we "do," that can't occur when we "don't." It's not too far fetched to suggest that doing something without emotions can produce emotions. So faking it until one makes it is not necessarily a bad strategy.

With that in mind here are two lists to make and do that will help you increase on the inside.

List #1: Demonstrate love

Think of how you can demonstrate love to the people and the world around you. Start with those persons and places closest to you and move out from there.

List #2: Make Peace

Make another list of activities, places, people or events that produce strong feelings of peace inside of you. When you think of peaceful surroundings what places come to mind? Or when contemplating activities that bring you peace what do you think of?

Now, with lists in hand, go and do!

15
OVERCOMING THE DO-DOS

Speaking of "dos," do you remember this past January? Yeah, the one where you had that day of crystal clear clarity, where everything came together, and you sat down and wrote that to-do list we call New Year's resolutions? Sound familiar? Good. Now pull out that list and let's review it. Go ahead. I'll give you a minute to get it. Maybe another minute or two? Or, uh, maybe not. Those darn resolutions are easier to write than to find.

I've made those lists before—the ones where I've put some time and effort into identifying what should be done to improve things in my life—and generally they're pretty solid lists. The problem is somewhere between punctuating the last bullet point and checking off the goal as DONE something gets lost. Either my will to do, my energy to do or that darn to-do list itself will be exhausted, preempted or misplaced and I will have entered the do-do zone: that state of being where I don't do what I know I should do and I do what I know I shouldn't do.

This isn't anything new. Most people understand this. Why is it then that if so many know so few do? Why is it that what we want to do we don't do and what we don't want to do we do? We start out great but can't finish. We have the best intentions but limited productions. We think positive thoughts but still get negative results. Why?

This is a classic case of living the do-dos and it's nothing new. This gap between what we know and what we do has been around for thousands of years for humanity and in our lives for however long you and I have been alive and it's not because of the new technology, television, violent video games, gangster music or any other modern excuse for why we're missing it.

Everything works, but not everything works forever.

The problem is not that I don't know enough; the problem is that I don't do what I know I should do. Our challenge is to find a way to narrow or close this knowing-doing gap and quit seesawing back and forth.

Paul the Apostle, the one who wrote most of the Christian Bible's New Testament, said the same thing long before any of us started wasting our lives watching reality shows on television. His question basically was who will save him from this constant back and forth, doing, not doing, doing and not doing some more?

His solution was found in God and I personally believe that without that spiritual connection finding the way is incredibly difficult if not impossible.

As in all the aspects of living *pono* I have good days and not so good days with happiness and health. There are times when I'm firing on all cylinders and others where I can't seem to find the keys much less put them in the ignition to start. I try to observe and learn from both the good and the bad, making notes along the way.

Keep in mind that "everything works, but not everything works forever." Just because something worked for you in the past doesn't mean it's going to keep working and producing. You may start out walking or jogging and lose twenty-five pounds. Great! That's good, solid work. Obviously, though, you won't go on losing weight until you disappear. At a certain point you'll hit a plateau, a place in your personal health development where there's not a lot of movement in any direction.

Before you get stuck in the flats again by the power of your own positive habits, recognize the lack of movement and reevaluate your behaviors and actions. Sometimes we get so comfortable we don't understand the danger. A "sense of comfort" is not on the list for describing a life that is categorized by *pono*. Our goal is not comfort but power to sustain us in achieving our purpose.

If a *Sense of Power* can be measured by looking at our happiness and health it stands to reason that if we provide ways to sustainably generate and increase these two components our power base will grow as well.

Being balanced physically, mentally, relationally and spiritually is a part of being *pono*. When we're in a right place, when our lives reflect alignment in our *Sense of Place, Purpose* and *Power*, we add the doing and producing to the knowing.

Less time in the do-do's and more time in the abundant life is the objective, and living *pono* is the way to get there.

KAʻALA SOUZA

16
YOU MUST BE THE GOOSE

Do you remember the story of the goose that laid the golden eggs?

I don't remember all of it but I do remember that some guy had a special goose that, instead of laying the regular old breakfast eggs, produced spectacular eggs of solid gold! Day after day, this fowl laid and laid beautiful, shiny, sparkly, solid gold eggs.

The goose owner guy had it made. He had arrived! No longer would he have to slave away, day after long dreary day at the goose farm. He would be living in style now! He was a rich man.

Things went on like this for a while until one day the guy had one of those bright ideas that everyone reading the story knows is going to blow it and ruin things for him. Instead of waiting every day for this goose to lay her one solid gold egg, he would kill the goose, open her up and pull out all the eggs!

Even if you've never read the story you can probably guess what happens in the parable.

Yep, once he'd killed the goose, he found out that there was no secret golden egg storage spot and that he had literally killed his chances for future riches. (As an aside, looking back on the story, you have to wonder what this guy was thinking. How big was this goose? Did he think she could carry around a hundred pounds of gold eggs and still walk?? I understand it's a parable/story and all but, still, really?? Unless he was a novice goose raiser he must have known that they only produce a single egg daily. Come on.)

I digress.

Your *Sense of Power*, or the absence thereof, is your goose. You are the goose!

Your ability and your capacity to produce is linked and tied to your physical, mental, relational and spiritual power base. Turn off those parts of you and your goose is cooked. (Sorry, couldn't resist.)

We look at the goose owner, shake our heads, and tut-tut at his foolishness all while slowly killing our own goose through neglecting our health.

Even if you allow yourself to become weak in just one area, (say, you're work life is so busy you stop exercising, working out or hanging out with your friends) you will cripple your ability to achieve and accomplish your goals and purpose. Maybe it won't show immediately but show it will.

It all works together and we can't escape it forever. We can get away from paying the bill for a little while but eventually that tab comes due. Think about all your efforts to get happy and healthy as an early bonus discount on that bill. Get more for your life.

HIGHLIGHTS

A *Sense of Power* combats the the "Drag of Flat," the absence of movement and motivation, through constantly maintaining and refilling the twin tanks of health and happiness.

A *Sense of Power* is also a sense of the spiritual.

Happiness is a skill that can improve or deteriorate. Use it or lose it!

Strength is the sum capacity of physical, mental, relational and spiritual strength and power.

The cycle of *pono* is living in a system of continuous creation and re-creation that allows us to fuel and achieve our purpose and mission.

If a *Sense of Power* can be measured by looking at our happiness and health it stands to reason that if we provide ways to sustainably generate and increase these two components our power base will grow as well.

Our goal should be to spend less time in the "do-do's" and more time living *pono*.

Your ability and capacity to produce is linked and tied to your physical, mental, relational and spiritual power base.

QUESTIONS

1. Currently, on a scale of 1-10, how strong is your *Sense of Power*?

2. Describe periods when your strength tank has been at the emptiest and the fullest. What were the differences in those periods?

3. Which area of health (physical, mental, relational, spiritual) is historically your strongest and weakest?

4. What activities can you do to strengthen each power area?

PART V: *BEING*

"You're packing a suitcase
for a place none of us has been
A place that has to be believed
to be seen."
–Bono, "Walk On"

"For what is a man profited,
if he shall gain the whole world,
and lose his own soul?
or what shall a man give
in exchange for his soul?"
–Matthew 16:26

KAʻALA SOUZA

17
ARE WE PONO?

Pops was sitting across my dining room table, staring me in the eyes and waiting for an answer to his question. My father-in-law can be an intense man and this was an intense question.

"Are we *pono*?" he asked me again.

This was one of only a handful of times we've actually had this kind of sit-down, serious conversation and the only time he's ever asked me this question.

Pops is a man for whom family is everything. He would do anything and give anything for all of us and one of his biggest desires was to make sure his family was healthy and whole—that we were all *pono* with him and with each other.

It was about three or four months ago, as I'm writing this, that Pops and my mother-in-law, Millie, came over to our house for a holiday visit. The visit itself wasn't unusual; over the past twenty plus years I've known him, Pops has been an active and frequent part of our family. Even after they moved to another island he would still fly down for weekend soccer games, school show recitals, birthdays and Christmases.

This one, though, this trip, was different. We all knew it. It wasn't the occasion or time of the year, it wasn't because of the holiday season. I wish. This trip was different because it would be his last.

Pops was diagnosed with cancer a while back and it's become progressively worse and more painful for him. When the doctors indicated that the cancer was in its later stages he moved back to Hawai'i from Florida to live his last days on the *'āina* and in the culture he loved.

He was always in top physical condition, always ready to take his grandchildren on hiking adventures, fishing trips and long bike rides, so it was a shock for me to see him at anything less than full strength. The cancer and treatment had done a number on him. The plane trip itself was almost too much for him to physically handle.

There's a strength in him, though, that is almost elemental and that no cancer could ever take away. He would hate it if I got all soft and gushy here but this strength is born out of his deep aloha for his family and his deep commitment to living *pono*.

"Are we *pono*?" he asked. "Are we good? I know I've made some mistakes along the way and don't want to die without making sure that things are right with us."

It was a question that only someone intrinsically *pono* would even ask.

He wasn't sitting back with his *Sense of Place, Purpose* and *Power* manufacturing correct responses out of the blue. The question came from a lifetime of choices and decisions, some good, some bad, motivated by what's right. Pops is an example to me of a life lived striving to be *pono*.

No one's perfect. Pops would be the first to tell you he's far from it. No one will ever be perfect, not in this world at least. But what we strive for, what we work towards, is a sense of rightness that permeates every aspect of our lives. We take our shots, hit or miss, we win or we lose, but we do it with the desire to be *pono*.

Are we *pono*?

Pops's question is one that each of us needs to pose of ourselves. It takes courage to ask and strength to answer. To be *pono* with the outside we need to also be *pono* on the inside.

Are we living the life we were meant to live, in alignment with our past and future, right with the people around us, solid with a strong *Sense of Power* flowing in and through our world? When we can answer in the affirmative then, and only then, are we truly and fully living.

I drove Pops and Millie to the airport. He told me that he wanted his ashes scattered in the ocean, out past the island he and my boys used to paddle out to for their fishing days. He told me that he wanted the song from Israel Kamakawiwo'ole, In This Life, playing as we did it. He told me that what he really wanted was his entire family, together, with no cracks, stressed or broken pieces, to be whole.

As we stood on the sidewalk I thanked him and told him he was more father to me than father-in-law. I told him that he had given me a benchmark to follow as a parent and grandparent. He was, and still is, my role model of someone living and being *pono*.

I was crying as they left, recognizing that all this talk of *pono* is just that—talk. There's an old Hawaiian saying that I've heard directed to me way too often that says *A'ole waha wale no*, meaning "that's enough talk already."

Pops taught me, without lecture or lessons, without talking about it, that until it's lived and lived fully, *pono* is flat out meaningless—it's academic. We must, I must, live *pono* to be *pono*. And that's meaning-FULL.

We're good, Pops. You and me, we're solid, we are *pono*.

KA‘ALA SOUZA

18
BOTTLES AND SHOVELS

Live *pono*

That's it; that's the solution. Easy, eh? Not really. The problem is that sometimes our minds are set in concrete ruts that we can't break out of and changing them is going to take a demolition team. So what then? The solution is easy to say and incredibly difficult to do.

In Hawaiian, the word *pono* literally means order, the correct and right order for things in our life. It has to do with alignment, balance, that which is correct and righteousness.

The solution to the problem we've been describing is *pono*.

Well, actually living *pono*. It's where those right things that we talked about earlier are in the right place, at the right time, in the right way and for the right reasons in your life.

Notice I didn't say the solution is in buying this book or program. It's not even just reading it. It's applying and doing—it's living it.

The secret to balance is really no secret. Figure out what really matters to you, design and build accordingly. No one but you can do this. The only problem is you're too busy working "in" your life to be able to step back and work "on" it. Many people spend more time planning their kitchen than their lives and it shows. It's time to do.

Live pono.

Pono is knowing, recognizing, remembering where and who we've come from, our *Sense of Place*. This place is an unmoving anchor for our identity. It's a place that is an understanding and acceptance of our past that frees us to move consciously and deliberately into the future. A *Sense of Place* is having a confident grip on who we are now as we stretch and reach into who we can be.

Live pono.

When we live *pono*, we live in a state of deliberateness, with our actions and behaviors, our thoughts and aspirations flowing from a position of awareness of our purpose in this world. This *Sense of Purpose* is *pono* and it stands counter to Thoreau's masses living in quiet desperation and going to the grave "with the song still in them."

Our purpose is to release the song in us that only we can sing. No one else in the entire world can sing it for us. When we live *pono* we release the melody and the harmonies that have the power to change our lives in this world and this world with our lives.

Live pono.

Balance, and the lack of balance, is evident and obvious in our lives. When the physical, mental, relational and spiritual parts of us are aligned and strong we are *pono*. There's a feeling of strength that we recognize and exude that is a our *Sense of Power*. When we are *pono* there is fullness and when there is fullness there is *pono*.

We are ready.

100 Billion Bottles

Where you are now is a result of where you were, what you did and what you thought yesterday and the day before and the day before that. Your current reality is a result of your past mentality. If this is true, and you want to change and transform your future, you must do something different today to affect tomorrow. If you're happy with where you are, you've made it, you've realized the full potential in your life, then don't change anything. You have a formula, you have a routine, stick to it and maintain it.

If the status quo isn't for you then you've probably tried different programs, plans and approaches and this book is probably another one of them. My biggest fear is not that you would read this book and not like it but that you would read it and not make a choice. Even if you read everything and despised it and said you're never doing A but instead will be doing X I'd be thrilled that you made a decision, made a choice, and are heading for a change.

> **Your current reality is a result of your past mentality.**

One of my favorite bible verses says that we are to not conform to the patterns of the world but instead we are to be transformed by the renewing of our minds. This is an incredibly powerful concept. Our minds got us to where we are now, thinking like the rest of the world, and our minds can get to where we need to be, thinking and living in abundance, in *pono*, the way we are supposed to be.

There are too many people not living with a *Sense of Place, Purpose* and *Power*, too many not living *pono*. Sting and the band The Police wrote about something like this in the song "Message in a Bottle" where he sees a 100 billion bottles washed up on the shore, all bearing the same rescue note. It seems he is not alone in being alone.

The chorus chants the line "I'll send an S.O.S. to the world" over and over again, almost like a child, sitting on that island beach, arms wrapped around their knees, rocking to and fro, hoping someone, anyone, gets the message.

The answer for us, for all of us, is not going to be found anywhere else but within us. There really is no rescue crew on their way to make things right. Way back in the beginning of this book I shared a Hawaiian proverb,

Aia no ka pane i loko iho no

that means the answer is found deep within us. It was placed there from the beginning. Our life, the quality of our life, is dependent on our ability to dig deep, uncover and discover it.

I hope in some small way this book can be a shovel, a response to your bottle and a help to find your answers.

Aloha.

Made in the USA
San Bernardino, CA
07 August 2015